D1013088

The Climb
of My Life

THE

CLIMB

OF

MY LIFE

Scaling Mountains with a Borrowed Heart

KELLY PERKINS

ROWMAN & LITTLEFIELD PUBLISHERS, INC.

Lanham • Boulder • New York • Toronto • Plymouth, UK

ROWMAN & LITTLEFIELD PUBLISHERS, INC.

Published in the United States of America
by Rowman & Littlefield Publishers, Inc.
A wholly owned subsidiary of The Rowman & Littlefield Publishing
    Group, Inc.
4501 Forbes Boulevard, Suite 200, Lanham, Maryland 20706
www.rowmanlittlefield.com

Estover Road
Plymouth PL6 7PY
United Kingdom

Distributed by National Book Network

Copyright © 2007 by Kelly Perkins

All rights reserved. No part of this publication may be reproduced, stored in
a retrieval system, or transmitted in any form or by any means, electronic,
mechanical, photocopying, recording, or otherwise, without the prior permission of the publisher, except by a reviewer who may quote passages in a review.

Cover quotes from Kelly Perkins interview with Katie Couric and Candice
Bergen on The Today Show. Copyright 2002 by MSNBC Interactive News,
LLC. Reproduced with permission of MSNBC Interactive news, LLC via
the Copyright Clearance Center.

Library of Congress Cataloging-in-Publication Data

Perkins, Kelly, 1961–
    The climb of my life : scaling mountains with a borrowed heart /
  Kelly Perkins.
      p. cm.
    ISBN-13: 978-0-7425-5877-9 (cloth : alk. paper)
    ISBN-10: 0-7425-5877-0 (cloth : alk. paper)
    1. Perkins, Kelly, 1961– 2. Mountaineers—United States—
  Biography. 3. Women mountaineers—United States—Biography.
  4. Heart—Transplantation—Personal narratives. I. Title.
  GV199.92.P473A3 2007
  796.522092—dc22
  [B]   2007015933

Printed in the United States of America.

∞™ The paper used in this publication meets the minimum
requirements of American National Standard for Information
Sciences—Permanence of Paper for Printed Library Materials,
ANSI/NISO Z39.48-1992.

To Craig,
my unconditionally loving husband,
who lifts me up to heights
not possible in the physical realm.

Contents

Acknowledgments

I OWE my deepest gratitude to my donor as without her, my life, let alone this book, would not be possible. In the same breath, I want to include my donor's family for carrying out her wishes, a critical component to the transplant process.

I want to thank my pretransplant doctors, Dr. David Cannom and his associates at L.A. Cardiology, for helping me believe there was life below the end of my rope. Equally, I share appreciation for my post-transplant doctor, Dr. Jon Kobashigawa and his colleagues at University Cardiovascular Medical Group, for not just keeping me alive, but instead finding ways to facilitate my lifestyle of climbing and traveling. I also want to recognize all the nurses, technicians, and staff I met along the way who provided comfort and genuine care, not only to me, but also to my family.

It's been a privilege to work with Cris Sumbi and Eric Marton with the California Heart Center Foundation (formerly Gift of the Heart Foundation) in supporting my ongoing commitment to Organ Donor Awareness. Furthermore, I want to extend my gratitude to Diane Tolzman, Richard Miller, and the entire team at Astellas (formerly Fujisawa Health Care) whose support resulted in an inspirational message that equaled any leading edge medication.

I would like to extend my appreciation to Tom Faye and Murlina Norwood at Bank of America for tailoring my position to work within the confines of my health limitations.

Thanks to all my mentors, mountain guides and/or teachers whose individual contributions have made for rich, adventurous, and most of all safe expeditions. These people include, Ranger Larry Sweet, Asano Otsu, Bob Gaines, Bobby McKenna, Honest Kessy, Wilbard Mijna, Bernard Shirima, Bethwel Mtui, Scott Stowe, Ken Yager, Kevin Thaw, Jean Pavillard, Tim Brown, Cedric Zulauff, Nick Cradock, Milo Gilman, Dave and Emma Medara, Jorg Wilz, Bob Falkenstein, Diana Christinson, and Suzy Gill.

Thanks to Brendan Riley and all the Bureau Chiefs at the Associated Press around the globe who have embraced the story. As well, to Michael Brown, his associate David D'Angelo, and the team at Serac Adventure Films who have redefined a "Kodak" moment.

A personal thanks to our longtime family friend, Jim Cheetham, for being such an enthusiastic supporter and amazing craftsman of the most beautiful charms a girl could ever imagine.

I commend the work of blood and organ donation advocates who set the bar high with passion behind their actions, including Andy Tookey (New Zealand), Dean Eller (USA), Lauren Larsen (USA), Jacques Pirenne (Belgium), and others who inspire me to continue my efforts.

Thanks to my many product sponsors, most of all, Scott Bowers at Oakley, for recognizing my goals and passions early on and championing my efforts.

My gratitude to Irwin Tenenbaum for taking a personal interest in my project and counseling me through the wild and crazy entertainment industry.

In regards to this book, I would like to recognize the late Richard Carlson for his insight into the literary world. (Also, his wife Kris, for standing strong during a period of immense grief and donating his organs following his unexpected death.) To Mark Chimsky who helped me get my arms around my story, Jennifer Horsman for encouraging me to sit down and write this manuscript after years of delays, Christopher Loudon for smoothing out the rough edges, and John Loudon for recognizing this story as a "diamond in the rough."

To my family and friends, my parents, Jere and Carol Williams for their indefatigable love and companionship during the best and worst of times; Craig's parents, Barbara and Ray Perkins, for amassing everyone's faith and keeping the numerous candles lit, while not burning down all the churches; the late Jake Fisher (Grandpa) whose compassionate legacy helped mold Craig to be a loving husband and caregiver; my dear friends TJ Nelson, Susan Kjesbo, and others too numerous to mention, for their gift of friendship.

And finally, where mere words are not enough to express, to my husband, soul mate, and self-proclaimed number one fan, Craig. For recalling and capturing the numerous life events as they occurred, and more importantly, for maintaining his patience, humor, endless enthusiasm, and creativity resulting in what turned into a "real-life fairy tale."

CHAPTER 1

A Life of Surprises

CRAIG could always keep a secret, but this one literally touched my heart.

The wind was howling, yet I couldn't hear a thing—not even the intense sobs that produced my steady stream of tears. A protective silence engulfed my heart, mind, and soul. I was in disbelief, overwhelmed by the magnitude of the moment. It was mid-July 1998, and Craig and I had been ascending Japan's Mt. Fuji, a grueling challenge that involved two long days of steep, unforgiving terrain. Minutes earlier, just before the celebrated "rising of the sun," my worn leather boots hit the mountain's summit. I felt a joyous sense of accomplishment, especially knowing this was no small feat for a heart transplant recipient.

After nearly a year of planning and training, we hoped and prayed that my standing on Mt. Fuji's peak might in some way lift the country's cultural veil and brighten the future of heart transplantation. Timing was perfect. Archaic Japanese laws regarding death had just been altered. At last recognizing brain death, they no longer considered a stopped heart the sole determination of death. This tremendous change meant the possibility of renewed life for countless existing and future Japanese citizens whose only chance for survival would be through the gift of a new heart.

Yet as I stood atop this symbolic shrine, the mission of my sacred trek was upstaged by the emotional bombshell that Craig had just revealed to me. He had tenderly placed a small leather pouch in my icy hands. Inside was what once embodied the life now beating within me.

Speechless, I held my donor's precious ashes.

For Craig, the element of surprise elevates the extraordinary to the fairy-tale realm. He has been uniquely skilled at creating magical moments ever since we first started dating. During our early years together, Craig's gift for spontaneous charm was best demonstrated when we shared a seemingly ordinary trip, a dozen summers earlier in Hawaii. I recall with fond memories the exact instant.

"That's perfect!" Craig said as he adjusted the zoom on the camera. "Don't move."

He set the timer and quickly ran to where I sat poised at the very top of Mt. Haleakala's volcanic crater, 10,000 feet high. It was five in the morning, and the sky crackled red and orange as the sun began to rise above the sparkling water far below. The dawning light cast the terrain of the mountain black, barren, and moonlike. Craig wrapped his long legs around my waist and, as we waited for the flash, he pulled out a velvet bag. Inside was a ring.

"Will you marry me?" he asked.

My heart skipped a beat, then another, then another.

Emotions raced through me as his words tumbled out. Negating his well-earned college reputation as a smooth "politician," Craig actually sounded nervous and tongue-tied, until he read the response in my eyes.

New love, new lives, endless possibility—this was our time. On the morning of May 23, 1987, we were married in St. Mary's church in downtown San Francisco, the same church where Craig's parents and grandparents had exchanged their vows. The perfect day promised a future of wedded bliss.

From the age of five to the day I left for college I lived on the border of Nevada and California, in Lake Tahoe. The mountains belong to me; my very being depends on forested hillsides, snowcapped peaks, an abundance of clean water and air, and the active lifestyle mountains provide. Wild places and breathtaking vistas are my church.

Our families shape us all, more or less, for better or worse. I have an older brother, and younger twin brothers. Each was a gifted athlete, and organized sports became my family's all-consuming priority. Their games overshadowed my childhood. Since most of the parental attention focused on the boys' activities, I turned inward and cultivated a strong sense of self-reliance, which over time lead me toward individual and noncompetitive outdoor interests. The mountains readily provided this. I was shy and introverted, and developed a fear of being unfavorably compared to my star brothers. I constantly held myself back and ignored opportunities. I became increasingly inhibited. Of course, with minimal involvement in anything remotely requiring athleticism, I was less than coordinated. My brothers relentlessly teased me, and every time I got the slightest bruise or flesh wound, they further fed my negative self-image by proclaiming me downright clumsy. "Kelly needs to wear a helmet 24/7!" they'd laugh.

What little ego I had left disappeared completely by age fourteen as I began to pack on the pounds. Thanks to a sedentary year doing little more than cheering my brothers on, combined with my newly hormone-charged body and, not to be overlooked or excused, excess eating, I gained an extra twenty-five pounds. To my growing dismay, on my tiny frame, the added weight was hard to conceal. My brothers thought they would have the last word with "Kelly-belly," but I showed them.

As with many young girls, the adolescent sting hit hard and fast. As quickly as the weight went on, I took it off. It was the beginning of a disciplined lifestyle that I have maintained ever since. During this awkward stage, I changed my mindset and focus. While I still avoided group or competitive sports, I committed to trying more independent activities that avoided any potential judgment. As my activity level increased, the added pounds disappeared. I found two passions, hiking in the summer and skiing in winter. This was Lake Tahoe, after all. It's what we do. While I had always skied, I took it to new heights. Before I hit sweet sixteen, you couldn't get the skis off me. I had finally arrived.

Growing up, I always had a job. The one I loved most was working for my dad at his young but growing civil-engineering company. Being the boss's daughter, my schedule was rather flexible, as homework always came first. Also, I was able to work outside, either counting cars for traffic studies or assisting surveyors in the field.

By the end of summer in 1977, I had earned enough money to buy my own car, a bright yellow VW bug with a sunroof. It sat in the driveway, waiting for that special day when I reached one of the most important teenage milestones; the day I got my driver's license. While the act of getting my license seemed so grown up, it was signing my donor card that demonstrated my true level of maturity. I chose to be an organ donor after my tumultuous junior year of high school, when I experienced the tragic loss of two classmates. The first was my dear friend Lisa who had been a passenger in her sister's car when they hit black ice on the highway, causing the car to skid off the road and crash, leaving her in a coma that she never came out of. Just months later, my friend Tony died instantly when he ran into a chain fence, and was nearly decapitated, while riding a motor bike through heavily forested woods. But, in all honesty, the reason I chose to be an organ donor wasn't just because I was so deeply affected by these deaths. I simply thought it was the right thing to do.

After high school I was off to college at the University of Oregon in Eugene. I chose U of O because it wasn't small and conservative, like Tahoe, but wasn't too big or intimidating either. The town of Eugene had a subtle earthy feel, with a 1960s overtone, balanced by the university's progressive, eclectic edge. It seemed homey but not stale. Because I am generally lighthearted and upbeat, I didn't think the wet weather would bother me, and might, if anything, provide added incentive to study. Besides this, I could see it was a Mecca for running, the perfect, time-efficient exercise for a college student.

Eugene is considered the heart of the running world, in part because of globally celebrated distance runner Steve Prefontaine's legacy, but also because it is the birthplace of the jogging craze that began back in the 1960s. Given the inviting labyrinth of trails through town and along the Willamette River, I quickly became swept up in the sport. Within weeks of arriving on campus, I bought my first pair of true running shoes and expanded my outdoor repertoire. Running became my outlet and daily exercise.

After two years contemplating Heath Sciences, my interest in nutrition surfaced. However, I had a little problem. The university did not offer such a program. As unlucky as this seems, it proved opportune. I needed out. The gun metal skies crushed my joyful spirit—it made me crazy. I didn't require constant sunshine, but needed a blue horizon every now and then. I felt entirely claustrophobic. Furthermore, I realized I had discipline but lacked stimulation. Despite Eugene's soulful small town charm, I could no longer live there. I longed for a change. Perhaps it was immaturity or my idealistic dream of a fairy-tale future, but I wanted a curriculum that would simply help prepare me for life and all that was coming. Initially I was open-minded, hoping I'd discover a passion for a subject that I could pursue professionally. But after completing my sophomore year I learned, or perhaps admitted, I wanted a college education more for the social experience—to grow as a person, rather than to lay the foundation for a career. My traditional upbringing, with a stay-at-home mom and a professional father, worked against any incentive for a career. Admittedly, I had a classic case of Cinderella Syndrome. I envisioned myself married to a suit-and-tie Prince Charming who worked nine-to-five while I was busy indulging in the rewarding aspects of being a mom. It didn't quite turn out that way.

In my junior year, I chose to transfer to San Francisco State University. I was familiar with the city. It was the escape destination of choice for my mom and I; the urban remedy for our frequent bouts of mountain fever. For us it was girl time, away from all the testosterone oozing through our house. The Bay Area seemed to bring balance to my isolated mountain upbringing. In Tahoe, my peers were strikingly homogenized, consisting almost exclusively of middle class Caucasian kids. Furthermore, due to strict building regulations and the extreme seasonal weather, the town was very conforming. As much as I loved the pine-studded mountains and what the Indians called the "big sky lake," there was only one main road—Highway 50. When I came off the mountain, from home or Heavenly Valley Ski Resort, I had no other choice. Highway 50 was it, left or right. Going straight you would find yourself in a very cold lake. I discovered a new enthusiasm in going to a big city, with streets jutting off every which way. But more than the streets themselves, I loved that they took you from one unique district to another, providing endless mazes of neighborhoods and colorful people. I was fascinated with North Beach, Little Italy, China Town, and Haight Ashbury, each with its rich, distinctive character. Warm sourdough bread on crisp mornings added to the heady mix of flavors. San Francisco State University did not offer a program in nutrition, but did have the most extensive Dietetics program in the Bay Area. I was under the gun to find a major that would honor the numerous science courses I had taken at University of Oregon. I didn't want to get caught in the vicious, expensive cycle of becoming a professional student. I already had the out-of-state transfer working against me, taking a significant step backwards with college credits.

San Francisco State was primarily a commuter school, and had a much different feel than U of O. Since SFSU lacked a youthful campus life, it was a natural decision for me to move in with my cousin Suzanne who lived near the USF (University of San Francisco) campus, just over five miles away. Suzanne shared a house with three roommates. One was moving out, leaving a vacant room for me. It was good fortune. I would be living a double life, SFSU for studies and USF for play. I mostly hung out with my roommates and joined in their extracurricular activities, specifically going to the school's basketball games. Despite my earlier aversion to team sports, I couldn't help but get caught up in the spirit and energy that particular season. USF was not only the hot team, but had one of the top ten players in the country. And so, at a USF basketball game, Craig said he spotted me for the first time.

Sitting in the bleachers a few rows below Craig, I was with Suzanne, whom he knew from the Fog and Grog, the campus pub. After the game, while I was temporarily distracted, Craig pulled Suzanne aside to get the skinny on me. "Who," he asked her, "is that girl you're with?"

Craig recalled I was dressed rather simply, wearing faded blue jeans, a blue-and-white-striped button down shirt, ponytail and no makeup—a casual, wholesome look he found attractive. When Suzanne commented I was from Lake Tahoe, she knew by his response she'd said the magic words. Given Craig's starry-eyed imagination, combined with his love for the mountains and passion for snow skiing, I perfectly fit his vision of the ideal girl. Although Craig was gregarious, he was rather girl-shy and asked Suzanne for an introduction. Being the good guy he is, Craig decided to wait until after the Christmas break to be formally introduced and ask me out, giving him time to first break off a long-distance relationship he'd been having with another girl. But he made a bold prediction about me that night while still in the gym bleachers, telling his friend David, "I am going to be dating that girl next semester."

When school resumed, Craig began stopping by my house on the pretense of visiting Suzanne, hoping he'd casually bump into me. Every time he stopped by, I wasn't around. But Suzanne would try to delay him, hoping I would return home. One afternoon, I happened upon an unfamiliar car parked in our driveway and a blond guy who looked like Craig approaching it, keys out, nonchalantly preparing to leave. I was thinking, "yes, show time, finally we meet!" I pulled my little blue MG convertible right up next to his car, got out, and offered a flirty "hello."

He politely acknowledged me, got into his car and drove off, just like that! I was utterly perplexed. After all his failed attempts, we finally run into each other, and what does he do? He bolts! Matchmaker Suzanne was equally confused. So, when the phone rang that evening, Craig was the last person I expected to hear on the other end of the line.

He introduced himself and said, "I stopped by your place today and no one was home."

"I know," I responded. "I saw you in the driveway and said hello." There was a long pause on the other end.

Finally, he sputtered, "Was that *you* who pulled up in the MG?"

Laughable? Not quite. I was insulted, or perhaps more embarrassed. After all, he'd forgotten what I looked like! Then it dawned on me. I couldn't put the entire blame on Craig. Regrettably, over the semester break I had tried to update my look, swapping my "girl next door" pony-tail for a seemingly more sophisticated, yet less than becoming perm. Add to this the exaggerated effect caused by the wind vortex of my convertible, and my hair looked more like the Nevada state flower, the tumble-weed. Needless to say, I realized I must have looked quite different than the first and only time he had seen me at the basketball game two months earlier. I was a far cry from his memory of a simple and wholesome-looking mountain girl.

Despite the very bad hair day, we arranged to meet again, and have been together ever since. Our initial courtship was like cramming for a final exam. On our first date, we ended the evening sitting on a secluded bench on top of Lone Mountain, overlooking the city lights and USF campus. We took in as much as possible as quickly as possible, sharing our past, present, and future hopes and dreams. His charm intrigued me in a way I couldn't quite put my finger on. Craig was born in San Francisco and raised in Marin County, just north of the Golden Gate Bridge. He seemed better rounded, which I attributed to his vast exposure to the diverse cultural activities of the city. He also had characteristics similar to those I admired in my Dad, including strong values and a good sense of humor. The similarity continued with his intensely Catholic education, extending from grammar school through college. As much as Craig had a conservative foundation, I viewed him as worldly, what I credited to his early travel experiences in both South America and Europe. One distinctive difference from my more reserved dad is that Craig was Mr. Campus "social": outgoing on the surface, but privately independent, keeping company with a small circle of close friends.

Like me, Craig was a commuter student. He lived part time at home, part time at his fraternity house, and the rest with his grandparents, whose home was in convenient proximity to the university. While most guys thrived on the camaraderie of the fraternity, Craig preferred a balance of friends and family. He viewed his living arrangements with his aging grandparents as an opportunity to spend time with them, specifically, his Grandpa Fischer. Grandpa's magnetism, together with his happy and humble demeanor, provided a tailor-made role model for Craig, and deeply echoes Craig's own character. Fortunately for me, Grandpa was a compassionate and tender caregiver, a trait that Craig adopted. When Craig was a youngster, it wasn't medicine that got rid of a cold or flu; it was Grandpa's care. Faithful as a retriever, he was unconditionally devoted to his grandkids and would drive all the way from his office in downtown San Francisco to their home in Marin (a forty-five-minute trek) to watch over the sick. His magic remedy consisted of simple pleasures—a cold rag on a feverish forehead, a few of his favorite comic books, and grandpa's colorful reminiscing of the "good old days." The most valuable lesson Craig learned along the way was the importance of "just being there!" Later, Craig mastered this fine art.

For our second date, Craig serendipitously invited me to go to Carmel for the day. Just under two hours from the city, it was a relatively easy day trip. To add to the fun mood, I suggested we take my little blue MG convertible so we could put the top down and enjoy the fresh ocean air. We were on our way. It was nostalgic for me because as a kid, my family spent a lot of time, including nearly every Thanksgiving, in Carmel. The special, bohemian village was, with its quaint architecture, secluded court-yards, art galleries, and small cafes, not just charming, but also romantic.

Craig and I arrived in time for lunch at the corner deli. I shared with Craig that when I was a little girl, it was one of my family's first stops in town to get fresh bread, great mustards, and deli meats. My brothers and I would always gawk at the selection of what they called "fine" foods not found in our local mountain grocery store–turtle soup, and the most disgusting item ever pack-aged for human consumption, pickled pigs' feet. For old-time sake, while Craig was waiting for our sandwiches, I had to go over to this section just to confirm those hooves, looking like they'd been soaked in formaldehyde, were still there. Sure enough, I wasn't disappointed. A lit-tle grossed out, but not disappointed!

After lunch, we headed to the ocean at the foot of the village. It was a picturesque day—chilly, sunny, and clear—as we made our way down to the street's end where it steeply drops off to a mile-long, white sandy beach below. Craig is a lanky 6-foot, 2-inches, compared to my 5-foot, 2-inches. With his much longer stride, he set a fast walking pace. I hustled to keep up. Because we were holding hands, his little tugs helped me along until we reached the sand and were able to stop, rest a minute, and sink our feet into the warm pebbles. The day was flirty and playful. As evening began to close in on us, we made the decision to stay for dinner to complete the perfect day.

After lingering over a lovely meal, we started back. The beginning of the drive, filled with relaxed conversation, proved uneventful as we meandered along the four-lane highway toward Gilroy, the not-so-date-friendly Garlic Capital of the World. There wasn't much around, just farms, ranches, and small businesses locked up for the evening. The sky was pitch black, dotted with tiny, distant stars. We were going about our merry way when suddenly we hit an obstacle in the road—a tiny bump, most likely an innocuous pothole. That bump gave my little car enough of a shake that the headlights went out momentarily, then flashed back on. Craig was driving and he slowed down trying to prevent it from happening again. We drove slowly, hoping the MG would hold together. Sure enough, it happened—lights out again, then on again, then out, then on. I scolded myself, thinking I should not have suggested bringing this lemon of a car. It was always in the shop for one thing or another. How stupid of me to think it would run perfectly for this important date! The problem with the lights was difficult to pinpoint. We needed a mechanic. Because it was Sunday and late, there was no one around to look at it until the following day. We could not risk traveling beyond Gilroy, where the comparatively quiet four lanes turn into a more heavily trafficked six-lane highway, so we agreed it was best to pull over. Luckily, there was a grubby little roadside lodge (what I call a classic "Norman Bates" motel) up ahead. We stopped. At age twenty, this would be the first time either of us had shared a motel room with a date. Our lighthearted mood quickly changed. Suddenly, we were serious-minded strangers. It was awkward for me, and clearly, for him too. I would have been disappointed if he was accustomed to registering for a room, but the two of us as bumbling neophytes made the awkward situation even more agonizing. To make matters worse, Craig and I didn't have enough money for the room. Out of sheer desperation to get past the growing unease, I nervously slid the innkeeper my trustful father's Visa, silently rehearsing my Catholic girl justification for charging a motel room to his credit card! With one hurdle down, we now had to face the daunting sleeping situation. I didn't dare ask how many beds—that would be much too horrifying. We just had to go with it, walking the fine line between looking like we knew what we were doing and trying not to seem like unsophisticated hicks. It was our solid conversation that became our salvation, as it carried us through until the wee hours of the early morning, when we both finally drifted off to sleep. The next day, after Craig dropped me back at my house, I walked upstairs to be greeted by three stony roommates who were understandably furious with me for not calling. With all of the angst of the previous night, I foolishly did not think to call. Ultimately, most of the wrath fell on Craig, as they made it known to me they weren't fond of him. Despite our innocence, I was clearly in a predicament on all fronts.

Craig and I were young and in no rush to hasten our relationship, so we let romance progress at a friendly pace. We were as much buddies as lovers, sharing what I called a "funship." Once summer rolled round, I returned home to earn some money, and Craig decided to also search for summer work in Tahoe. He could stay at his other grandmother's vacation home in town, where he had spent time in past summers and winters. Having just turned twenty-one, he secured work at the High Sierra Casino. My job was across the street at Caesar's Hotel and Casino, but our schedules couldn't have been more different. Craig worked nights driving a limo, usually transporting VIP high rollers and celebrities from the Reno airport to the hotel and back. I worked the day shift as a waitress. Still, during breaks, before and after work, and on days off, we found time for each other. I was eager to experience a different side of Craig, to see how he coped in a mountain environment, my backyard wonderland. I knew he dressed up nicely and could be well mannered and affable, but I was thrilled to discover he was just as comfortable dressing down and getting grubby in the backcountry. That summer of 1982 would prove a memorable one, marking the true beginning of our courtship years and mutual love of the mountains.

Our first overnight camping experience was in Lake Tahoe's Desolation Wilderness, where we hiked to the majestic Lake of the Woods, 8,000-feet high, above the Upper and Lower Echo Lakes. The surrounding mountains still had plenty of snow, and the cobalt blue Tahoe sky was crystal clear. We trekked along a well-worn trail, a topography map in hand. When we finally reached our campsite, Craig quickly set up our tent and built a rock fireplace. For a guy who was raised in what many referred to as the "laid-back, hot tub capital of the world," he had intuitive backpack skills. I got an early sense of Craig's chivalrous nature when we went fishing and something started tugging at our fishing pole. Instead of claiming the prize himself, he handed the pole to me. As I landed a shimmering, sixteen-inch rainbow trout he proclaimed me a champion fisherman.

At summer's end, Craig introduced me to two of his college friends, Anne and TJ, who needed a third roommate for the flat they occupied near the USF campus. Because my cousin Suzanne and two other roommates had graduated, I needed to find a new place to live. It was propitious; I not only found a place, but also established an enduring friendship with TJ, who instantly became like a sister to me.

Craig's and my early years together was a time of exploration. We loved traveling and continued our exploits with college buddies, dividing our free time between hiking in the Sierras and visiting a favorite beach in nearby Bolinas, a great surf spot and remote 1960s throwback community in Marin. Locals have gone to great effort to maintain its quaint charm, discouraging tourists by periodically removing city signs that would otherwise direct people to the seaside town. At the beach, our days were filled with nonstop sports including paddleball, Frisbee, Hacky Sack and, for the boys, surfing. No wonder we were all so fit. Even after college, the friends who joined us on those sunny excursions remained a tightly knit group.

Our group beach trips subsided after college, but backpack expeditions in the Sierras became a festive annual event. With Craig organizing the details, our initial excursions were nothing short of playful as many of the beach toys found their way into our backpacks. Our activities included fishing, mountain Frisbee golf (using rock and tree features as holes) and, for me, climbing to the top of the nearest peak. My "peak-bagging" activities would later come to define my image. To add to the fun, inflatable rafts were introduced, which increased the weight in our packs, but no one complained. The tranquil luxury of floating in the middle of a high mountain lake was well worth the added pounds. It wasn't about being efficient and light, it was about bringing anything and everything that would amuse us. TJ and I would light-heartedly try and prove our strength, albeit at a cost. Our heavy loads created black-and-blue backpack imprints on our hips and shoulders. As unbecoming as the bruises were, we were proud to demonstrate that we were carrying our share, and that we were just as determined as the guys. My bruises became more acute, just short of flesh wounds, when Craig and I took this funfest to another level. On a few occasions, we added skis and boots to our packs with the goal of hiking high enough up in the peaks to snowfields that had dodged the summer heat. In spite of the rigorous nature of the outings and the resulting aches and pains, we all further bonded, solving one another's life issues and laughing our way through the wood-scented trails of the Sierra Nevadas.

As a graduation present to himself, Craig decided to take a six-week tour of Europe with our friend Mark. The trip, partly organized through the USF Business School, was divided between appointments with various companies in several different countries and backpack-style journeying. Craig returned with exciting accounts of their adventures, a fresh perspective, and wild stories that inspired me to do the same. I was on the five-year university plan, but was committed to make an overseas trip happen the following year. When it came time, I signed up with a national program called the AESU, Alumni World Travel. It was madness, seventeen European countries in thirty days, and an education that would rival college. Our travels apart even brought us closer together—it, too, was a shared passion.

In February 1986, three years after graduation, Craig decided he wanted a change. He had been working for Equitec, a real estate syndicate in the East Bay with numerous offices around the country. One of his responsibilities was opening satellite offices for the company's securities division. The travel opportunity exposed him to new places, fueling his desire to move. He had lived in the Bay Area his entire life and felt the urge to grow. To do so, he needed new surroundings. He had a business contact near Los Angeles for Grubb and Ellis, a commercial real estate brokerage company. Southern California looked promising and, after a successful interview and subsequent job offer, Craig was seduced by his first Newport Beach sunset. His perspective changed from "if" he made the move to "when." He called and said, "You have to come down and check this place out." I knew, deep down, where his heart was. Yet, he was respectful in not rushing the decision without assessing my willingness to join him. I struggled with leaving the Bay Area because it was just beginning to feel like home to me. But it was time to look to the future. I wanted to love where I lived, but I needed to live with the one I loved. Maybe it was my casual nature, but I didn't think the move was too risky. I was not, after all, talking about a permanent facial tattoo. If the move wasn't right, I could simply return. And the idea of a fresh beginning, in a place full of new things and people to discover, was tantalizing. My intrigue was peaked, and in no time I was on my way south to see what all the fuss was about. Craig had surveyed the area for rental units and amenities, and proved quite the shrewd tour guide when I arrived. He had my stay planned to the minute; from beautiful drives to quaint beaches to romantic restaurants. His excitement was contagious. I was sold. Craig accepted the job and immediately put a moving plan in motion. To be prudent, as we were quickly handing our savings over to the phone company, we decided I would move down as soon as Craig got settled. Our separation was brief but miserable. Each day felt like a week, each week like a month. We desperately missed one another. Finally, in April, I headed south.

Craig secured an apartment on the Newport Beach Peninsula with our friend Mark, his college and European backpack crony. To make my adjustment easier, though much to my parents' chagrin, I temporarily moved in. We were a happy household, sharing similar hours and a compatible lifestyle. Mark was our perfect roommate and playmate. He surfed late afternoons into the sunsets with Craig and, in the mornings, joined me to run the beach strand before work. This continuation of our active lifestyle helped us ease through the transition from college to the real world, and we all made it a priority to balance work and play.

Living on the peninsula, I began to take an interest in water sports, eager to take advantage of my proximity to the ocean. I also wanted to have another sport to share with Craig, whose natural love for the water would classify him as part fish. I was constantly teasing him that my advanced evolution no longer required I live in water to survive. Truth was, though I'd grown up in the reflection of one of the most beautiful lakes in the world, I had a fear of water. Yes, some of my favorite childhood memories were of the lake and our family boat, but I was never eager to jump into the ice-cold mountain runoff. For several summers, before my brothers' baseball schedule became all-consuming, Mom and Dad would pack us all up, motor out to the middle of the lake, and let us take turns water skiing as we made our way to Emerald Bay for weekend picnics. Skiing was really the only water sport I'd ever tried, and only because the goal was to stay on top of the freezing water, not to go in it. It had been a long while since I had been in any deep body of water. The last time was a dare to jump into an icy mountain lake. Just the thought of it still takes my breath away. The ocean intimidates me even more. I fear the strong currents will suck me under and sweep me away.

I set a new goal for myself; I made a commitment to get wet. I decided to try scuba diving. I figured if there was any water sport to help overcome my fear, this had to be it. I would be fully submerged, on purpose, for a long period of time. I signed up for a local class in Laguna Beach, and worked on my water skills through a number of practice sessions in a pool. As expected, I was the group's only timid swimmer, further feeding my fear and lack of confidence. But, I hung with it. When time came to visit the ultimate testing ground, the ocean, it was a disaster. First of all, my clumsy entry, trying to balance myself amongst the pulling and crashing waves while loaded down with thirty-five additional pounds of gear and awkward flippers, was neither easy nor pretty. My gracelessness soared to new heights. Amazingly, I somehow managed to get beyond the beach break, even regaining enough composure and breath to venture underwater. As soon as my instructor swam over to have me clear my mask, one of the standard drills to get my PADI Certification, I freaked out and bolted to the surface. The first cardinal rule, reinforced time and time again, is *under no circumstances do you quickly ascend*. You can get decompression sickness, a life-threatening condition known as the bends. So far, not so good! After repeatedly disastrous tries, I gave up and made arrangements to come back another day to get "checked out." Luckily, the second day was a little better. I managed to pass; earning my certification while telling myself I would never do this again. Though the entire exercise was a flop and I failed to overcome my fear of water, it wasn't a total loss. I made the effort despite my trepidation. And the experience further clarified that no matter where I live, I am a mountain girl.

We returned to the Bay Area fairly often because our family and many of our friends were still there. In June 1986, we came up from Newport Beach for a quick visit before leaving for Hawaii, where Craig was serving as groomsman in a friend's wedding. My parents, who had recently purchased a second home across the bay, made the easy drive over to Marin to see us off before our trip. Unbeknownst to me, long before our move south, Craig had purchased an engagement ring and worked out a plan. He wanted to do the formal and proper thing, maintaining the tradition of respecting my parents and our relationship by asking them first for my hand. But Craig didn't have much time to do so, and I was always nearby. To get around this, Craig came up with a clever idea. His family owned a 1931 Chevy, which they fondly referred to as the "old car," complete with a two-person rumble seat that was most often used to transport neighborhood kids to the local ice cream parlor. Craig suggested that it might be fun to take my parents for a drive. As a ruse, he proposed driving each of them to a nearby building that he had been involved with during construction when he was working at Equitec. First, he puttered off with dad, then with mom. They returned, we fired up the BBQ, and sat down to dinner, with me none the wiser about what they'd really been up to. The next day, Craig and I left for Hawaii, where he would later unveil his romantic proposal atop Mt. Haleakala. We returned just over a week later, with a sparkle on my finger and the promise of a blissful future. Our fate was sealed.

Afterward, I learned Craig's conversation with my parents in the "old car" was rather comical. While my Dad maintained the more stoic role of a typically over-protective father upon learning of Craig's intentions, my mom was a bit more outwardly emotional. Of course, timing is everything. When it was mom's turn for her ride up to the building, Craig parked the car in the lot's most private corner, the same place he had only minutes earlier revealed his plans to my Dad. Upon hearing the news my mom immediately broke down crying. As Craig leaned over to give her a hug, they were hit with the high beam of a police flashlight. Both she and Craig looked up at an obviously alarmed policeman. Unbeknownst to Craig, the building site had become a popular "make-out" spot for local high school students. After a little explaining, the officer laughed and wandered off in search of more legitimate offenders.

Our engagement lasted eleven months, which was about eleven months too long for me. I had looked forward to being married ever since I was a little girl. Taking a modified traditional path, we thought it best to live separately until the big day. Craig had a real estate buddy whose girlfriend needed a roommate, so timing was perfect. But Craig and I remained inseparable, spending all of our free time together, and most of it with our friend Mark. We had the beach at our disposal all week long, so maintained weekends for our mountain fix, often leaving Friday evening for the High Sierras and not returning until late Sunday night.

To stay motivated, our getaways often had a goal-oriented theme. One such trip was a three-day mountain survival program in the middle of nowhere, California.

We lived off the land with just the clothes on our backs—no food, and no sleeping bags. The course was led by a gal who some would consider a fruitcake, or more specifically, a serial dieter. She used these extreme outings as a way to maintain her weight. While her starvation strategy took the guesswork out of calorie counting, I don't think her weight maintenance program will rival the popularity of the Zone diet any time soon. Still, the trip was worthwhile, as the lessons we learned later proved immensely valuable. We practiced skills essential for wilderness survival including building shelters, making fire beds, finding and purifying water, identifying edible plants, fishing with our hands, and navigation. As a one-time survival exercise it was a worthy experiment, but is one trip I would not be eager to repeat.

Another memorable trip that later proved fateful involved Craig, Mark, and myself setting out to hike to the top of Mt. Whitney in California's Eastern Sierras. We chose the peak because it is the tallest mountain in the continental United States, standing 14,496 feet. It was a terrifically challenging goal to work toward. While there is nothing technically difficult about the trail we took, many people underestimate the effects reduced oxygen at higher elevations have on the body. Though the three of us were equally fit and strong, Craig began to feel the ill effects of altitude as we ascended above the tree line. At 12,000 feet we dumped our gear at Trail Camp, our campsite for later that night and the last reliable source for water before heading on to the summit. We hoped our lighter loads would provide an added boost for our summit push, and offer a bit of relief to Craig's growing ailments. As we made our way up to the next significant milestone, a ridge that sits at 13,600 feet, our minds were focused on cresting the top and seeing the view on the other side. The only thing that separated us from this milestone was a formidable challenge—the infamous ninety-six switchbacks. About one-third of the way up this section, Craig slowed down, stopping frequently to rest, and finally hit an altitude wall. He insisted Mark and I continue on without him, saying he would catch up. But as Craig pushed himself to continue, he ultimately succumbed to the insidious effects of altitude sickness. He had reached the ridge at Trail Crest, the scenic milestone that welcomes you to Sequoia National Park and connects with the John Muir Trail. In spite of the spectacular view, he wasted no time in turning around. His bid for the summit had ended. Mark and I had no idea of Craig's intense misery as we continued our climb. The last two miles of the rocky ascent seemed really long as the trail faded into a boulder scramble to the summit. We stuck with it, and after what seemed like hours, finally reached the top. With the day closing in and Craig nowhere in sight, we headed back down to find him. When we finally arrived at camp, we found Craig with his feet sticking out of a half-erected tent filled with the overwhelming stench of vomit. I felt terrible; I hadn't realized how sick he was. Fortunately, he'd had the good judgment to turn around and get to a lower elevation. Craig woke early the next morning, feeling better. We quickly made our way down to the trailhead. When we reached the little store at the base of the mountain, Mark and I bought and proudly displayed patches that read, "I climbed Mt. Whitney." For Craig, I bought a consolation prize: a patch that read, "I ALMOST climbed Mt. Whitney." From the determined look on his face, I knew we would be back.

During our early years together, we continued to weave mountain treks into our busy lives. By choice we purposely delayed starting a family to further take advantage of such carefree and idyllic times. We very much wanted to have kids, but only after we'd quenched our insatiable thirst for adventure. Craig continued working as a commercial real estate agent while I took a job as a residential appraiser. Our schedules were flexible, and we were constantly drawn to the splendor of the mountains and hiking in the wilderness.

In 1988, just a year after we were married, we found ourselves breathless at the top of Mt. St. Helens in Washington. That tumultuous climb left an indelible impression on us as, ironically, it soon paralleled our lives. The trail had just opened a year earlier, permitting us to be among of the first wave of recreational hikers to be allowed up to the rim of the volcano since its eruption in 1980. The mountain was desolate, and at certain times we were knee-deep in ash as soft as powder. The rim overlooked Spirit Lake, and the water below was littered with huge trees that had blown off the mountain. From where we stood, the massive timbers looked like toothpicks floating atop the lake. Devastation was everywhere, and we felt the solemn power of nature all around us. Awestruck, I couldn't help but think of how everything had been reduced to ash, but out of the ashes would come new life. The mountain was merely acting out its part in a long history of cyclical changes. Releasing its core with such great force, the mountain is sharing riches that come from within—new soil, minerals, and life. Upon returning to the outer edges of the blast zone, I looked down with greater awareness and spotted a small patch of green emerging from the ash. Life was returning to the mountain. Slowly it would regain what was lost and perhaps be a little richer and healthier than before. Little did we know that the same sense of loss and renewal would soon echo within my own life.

CHAPTER 2

Airlift over the Matterhorn

B Y spring of 1992, Craig and I had put aside enough money for our version of a dream vacation, a month-long trip to the mountains and villages of Switzerland, Italy, and France to celebrate five years of wedded happiness. Traveling light, with a few belongings stuffed into small backpacks, we moved freely from town to town, swiftly navigating through unfamiliar places in search of interesting sights to absorb. We had a general sense of where we wanted to go each day, but depended on the locals for more specific ideas. Luck was often on our side, as we regularly happened upon cute villages with quaint bed and breakfasts that reflected both the local flavor and our romantically adventurous mood. With no specific agenda or reservations, living was easy as we casually followed whatever road looked most interesting.

We started in late April with a perfect day of spring skiing in Corvatsch, Switzerland. It was the final day of the season, the sky a rich blue and warm sun gleaming off the dramatic backdrop of the glacial-capped Alps. We schussed down wide-open runs dotted with stone huts strategically placed to entice adventurers in for a bit of mountainside refreshment. The crowds were thin. It was as though we'd stumbled across the best-kept secret in Europe, helping us believe this day was specially reserved just for us. Craig and I smiled at one another as an elderly couple, probably in their eighties, skied past us. I said, "That will be us at that age." Not missing a beat, Craig nodded in agreement. Lost in our reverie, we ended the day with a few too many après ski drinks as we toasted each of the numerous peaks that surrounded us. And this was only the beginning.

Taking advantage of the warmer weather, we decided to jump on a train to explore southern Italy. We opted for Sicily, correctly guessing it would compliment our desire of a unique travel adventure. Our first night's simple pizza dinner in the charming town of Taormina turned into a dining drama. We got what we came for—authenticity, from the mandolin music, food, and Chianti to two locals who looked like they'd been lifted straight out of *The Sopranos*. But Guido and Tony weren't Hollywood mobsters. Each was the legitimate (or, perhaps more accurately, *not so* legitimate) article. The Mafioso, we quickly learned, was as much a part of southern culture as the ancient ruins. As novel as this was, Craig and I were much more interested in the region's geothermal (volcanic) landscape, in which Mt. Etna was currently playing an active role. Mounting a Vespa, we motored toward the uninhabited Valle del Bove for a closer view. The mountain was moving, both literally and figuratively—jittered by hundreds of tremors each day. It seemed remarkable to us that the locals utterly ignored the mountain's constant grumbles as they busily went about their workaday lives in the surrounding valleys below. We roamed aimlessly through rolling hills of green, fertile countryside. Occasionally we came across a rancher alongside a weather beaten wooden hay cart, towed by his most beloved animal, a scene that seemed to set the clock back decades, even centuries. Needless to say, it provided a startling contrast to L.A.'s noisy, polluted urban sprawl.

Moving on, we traveled by boat to the remote and sparsely populated island of Stromboli. Here we had an opportunity to have an up close and personal experience with the island's life force. We ran into a few locals, who invited us to meet after lunch at the town's Cathedral to join a small group of trekkers who were going to hike to the crater's rim. The goal was to arrive at sunset, enabling us, as the darkness fell, to watch the mountain spew its fiery lava, the night sky ablaze. Once we were at the top, we were able to see the show from the comfort of heated seats—provided naturally by the starring attraction itself. A group of adolescent German students on a school-sponsored field trip had also made the trek, adding even more energy to an already explosive show. Just when we thought the experience could not be topped, the students led the way down the backside of the mountain with flashlights illuminating a trail against the pitched black sky. As their zigzagging beams gained momentum, the kids broke out in song. It was a delightfully bizarre Rodgers and Hammerstein moment, the romantic mood heightened by our very own personal choir.

Having fulfilled our Mediterranean adventure, including a short stint along the French Riviera where the Cannes Film Festival was in full bloom, we decided to head back to the mountains.

Zermatt was our destination of choice as it offered unsurpassed beauty and, most memorably, a close-up view of the world-famous Matterhorn. Looking up at the grand mountain, its sharp, pyramid-shaped ridges seemed so stately and distant as to be almost untouchable. It was obviously a climb reserved for only the most experienced mountaineers. My thoughts turned to the only person I'd ever met who had climbed the Matterhorn. His name was Uli. He was a wonderfully handsome Swiss man who owned a small ski and mountaineering store in Marin County where Craig and I together bought our first pair of hiking boots. As he turned and walked away to find our sizes, I noticed his muscular calves, testimony of his credentials. Listening to him reminisce, I could tell that this peak held a special place in his heart, a highlight in any serious alpinist-climbing career. Recalling Uli's memories of his thrilling experience, Craig and I looked up at the snow-frosted Matterhorn, awed by its magnificence and those daring to attempt such an ominous climb. While I idolized the mountaineers, laden down with rope and gear as they made their way through town to the classic peak, it seemed much too daunting. I was satisfied to simply hike among the wildflowers and streams in the mountain's shadow far below. For a peak bagger, the Matterhorn seemed the ultimate prize, but even I wasn't crazy enough to take on such a formidable challenge.

As I stood carefree in the center of one of nature's most spectacular settings, how could I know that this was the calm before a shocking tempest that would turn Craig's and my world upside down?

It started small, like a tiny flutter deep inside my chest. It had been just two months since we'd returned from Europe. I felt my normal, healthy self. I was feeling great, except for periodic nighttime episodes. Abed in the dark stillness, my heart began racing. I wasn't overly anxious but, like most people, I'd had no reason to "notice" my heart before. I went to my doctor to find out what was causing the palpitations.

It was July 1992, my last days of innocence.

After going through a routine test, he put his finger on my wrist to feel my pulse and counted perfect sinus rhythm, fifty beats per minute. I knew from my physical training that it was a good heart rate, and quite normal for a healthy, active thirty-year-old female.

"You're physically fine," the elderly doctor said, giving me his most reassuring smile. But as I was on my way out, he handed me a card advising me to schedule an appointment with a psychiatrist.

Baffled, I asked, "Why a psychiatrist?"

The doctor looked amused. "Because, I think you are stressed!"

If there's one thing I wasn't in those days it was stressed. It simply wasn't in my nature to worry. I took things in stride and, frankly, there wasn't much to worry about. Life was great. I was married to my soul mate, living in a laid-back beach community, and financially stable with a promising career. As I walked to the parking lot and opened the car door, I laughed a bit nervously to myself, thinking, "O.K., so maybe I'm nuts."

Yet the occasional bouts of a suddenly racing heart continued. Imagine sitting in an easy chair, book in hand and musing about what's for dinner, when your heart abruptly takes flight as if you were approaching the finish line in a 10K race.

One weekend, Craig spent a rare night away, traveling up the coast to Manhattan Beach with a few buddies for a surf-fest. I woke up in the middle of the night slumped near the toilet. Oh. My. God. How did I get there? What was I doing there? I had no memory of it!

I punched out the number to call Craig, but quickly hung up because it was still the wee hours of the morning. I waited anxiously by the clock and phone for the time to pass, knowing my call would wake a few others besides Craig. Finally, at 5:00 A.M., I made the call. From the grogginess of his voice, I could tell he was still half asleep. He rushed home. We tried to figure out what had happened—but neither one of us could make any sense of it. The recent EKG had said I was normal, so I didn't equate it with my heart. It had to be something, but what? I had no other symptoms.

I am fine now, I thought. I'll just worry about it another day.

Come September, we set about preparing for our tenth annual backpack trip with our college friends. Destination: Heart Lake—oh, the irony! The lake is nestled 10,000 feet up in the John Muir Wilderness area of the Central Western Sierras. I wanted to get in a run before we left, as I knew we'd be stuck in traffic most of the day. Craig never ran, but for some reason, decided to tag along this time. As we scooted around my usual midweek path, Craig, the once a year runner, took the lead as I progressively fell back, trying to find my breath. Unlike any of the other times I'd run this same route, I was extremely winded. My run slowed to a fretful walk. I motioned to Craig to go on. I tried to brush it off, blaming it on a bad night's sleep.

Later that same morning, I was in Laguna Beach inspecting a house for an appraisal. While walking the property, I felt strong palpations in my chest. It was unusual, and because it had been a few hours since I'd finished my run, it alarmed me. I wrapped up the job and headed back home along Pacific Coast Highway. As fate would have it, I passed my doctors office and decided I still had some time before meeting Craig at noon to pop in. His face registered surprise upon seeing me so soon after my last visit. I sheepishly asked him to listen to my heart, fearful that, once we'd departed for the mountains,

I'd be miles away from civilization. He hesitated, but agreed. After I undressed and put on my paper cover-up, a nurse came in to hook me up to electrodes for an EKG. As the machine started tracing peaks and valleys, the pattern looked more like a seismology reading of an earthquake than my "normal" heart strip.

Imagine my alarm as my doctor's voice quivered, "Your heart rate is 190 beats per minute."

He turned to his nurse, who looked as concerned as he did. "Stay right here with Ms. Perkins. I'll be right back," he said, returning moments later with the doctor from the adjacent practice. They both looked at the EKG strip, their faces filled with alarm. Knowing my previous resting heart rate had been 50, it didn't take a doctor to tell me that four times my normal rate was not a good thing!

The message was clear: I needed help and I needed it now.

The doctor immediately called Craig to come to the office, and then arranged for me to see a cardiologist at a nearby hospital for more extensive tests. One such test was an echocardiogram, which generated an image of the heart, much like a sonogram reveals an unborn fetus. Lying on the table, I looked over at Craig and, suddenly grasping the urgency of my situation said, "They need to hurry. We won't make our trip if it takes much longer." Impatience filled my voice, the frustration and confusion of a healthy person who cannot imagine anything different. The technician smeared my skin with lubricant and rolled the probe across my bare chest. After he finished, he said it would be about a half-hour before the doctor viewed the results. Instead of sitting in the waiting room, we took a short walk over to a local shopping mall.

It was my last thirty minutes of "normal."

When we returned, the nurse had a worried look on her face as she hurried us into a room. The cardiologist immediately admitted he was alarmed by what he saw. He attempted to explain what was wrong with my heart. He ripped the white, tissue-like paper guard off the examining table and drew a heart. "This is a healthy heart." He drew the two ventricles and atria. Then he drew another heart. "This is the picture we have of your heart." The left ventricle was blown out of all proportion. It looked like a balloon about to burst.

Something was obviously wrong! *But what?*

The cardiologist said, "We have to keep you overnight for observation, to monitor your heart." In spite of the doctor's visible concern, Craig and I remained in denial, thinking some silver bullet or special cure-all pill would make this escalating nightmare recede. Because I viewed this unexpected hospital visit as nothing more than a speed bump, I asked Craig to go home for my laptop so I could finish a few appraisals. When Craig returned, he called both our parents. Naturally, they were dumbstruck, not believing what they heard. My parents panicked. My dad said, "We're on our way." Craig then called TJ to let her know our plans had changed—we couldn't join the group for the weekend. She was shocked. In all these years she'd known us, we had never missed a backpack trip, especially one of our annuals. Her nursing background didn't help matters. She knew too much, and then let her vivid imagination run wild. She contemplated canceling the trip altogether, knowing she'd have no phone reception in the mountains and would be completely unreachable. Craig encouraged her to go with the group and, reluctantly, she finally agreed. I heard Craig say, "TJ, don't worry. We don't know enough yet, and I think the doctors just want to observe her. So, relax. She will be fine. Please, just go have a good time."

Craig stayed right by my side until it was time for bed. We said goodnight, and he headed home. As I lay there alone, all kinds of random thoughts ran through my mind. I was perplexed. I led a healthy lifestyle and had no family history of disease. I was sure it was no big deal, still convinced there would be a quick fix to solve the problem. With limited drug experience, I knew it would take more than a Tylenol, maybe an antibiotic or anti-inflammatory. I disliked taking any medication and preferred to "tough it out." But, in this case, if I needed to take a pill I would, just to put this all behind me. My mind continued to wander as I looked around the stale, antiseptic room. The eerie quiet made me nervous. I expected there'd be other people, but couldn't see anyone, including patients or even a nurse's station. This wing of the hospital was undergoing renovation, I could tell because the room numbers on the door were removed for painting. Silently, I wondered, "Am I the only patient in here?" The stillness was amplified. It seemed creepy, and I felt totally isolated. I grew frustrated, thinking this entire drill of "observing" me overnight seemed a complete overreaction. The first night I'd ever spent in a hospital wasn't for something wonderful like having a baby, or even for something routine. My heart, the heart of a fit, active thirty-year-old, was at risk. It all seemed like a bad dream.

I must have dozed, because I heard a sudden noise and woke with a flinch, pulled back into my miserable reality. I looked up at the stark room's sole piece of decoration; a wall clock indicating it was 4:00 A.M. To my surprise, a doctor dressed in a suit and tie entered the room. He introduced himself, "Hi Kelly, my name is Dr. Thomas. I am the head cardiologist of the hospital."

He gently pulled a chair to my bedside, and sat down. "We need to talk," he said solemnly, explaining, "We are a small hospital and not equipped to handle a *serious* situation like yours." My brain stopped at the word *serious*. "I have made arrangements for you to see a specialist at Good Samaritan Hospital in Los Angeles who is highly experienced in electrical issues of the heart and is much more capable of taking care of you."

My thoughts could not keep up with his words, and I struggled to understand what he was saying. I nodded my head as if I was following him, yet couldn't make sense of anything. The word electrical alarmed me. I thought of my old MG's chronic electrical problems and the mechanic's comment that electrical issues are always a puzzle and inevitably the most difficult to solve.

Just then, Dr. Thomas tightened his hand around mine and said, "We are going to transfer you right away by air." Oh my God. *By air*? An hour away? I maintained my composure until he left the room and then called Craig. As soon as I heard his voice, I broke down.

Craig hustled into the room and leaned over to give me a kiss on the forehead. The look on his face told me how deeply worried he was. We now knew it was serious. A few hours later, the helicopter team arrived and quickly transferred me to a gurney to prepare me for the flight. Craig was told he needed to drive separately, as there was only room for the pilot, two EMTs and me. I didn't want Craig to leave. He stayed as long as he could, holding my hand and walking alongside my gurney as I was wheeled to the roof. As we neared the helicopter, Craig stepped back and watched while they secured me in place. I felt nauseous, like I had been kicked in the stomach, an awful feeling mirrored on Craig's terrified face. I desperately wanted him with me and couldn't wait to be reunited in L.A.

Everyone in the helicopter was cheery. Their goal was to keep me calm. The pilot said, "Let's bank over Disneyland and see if you can catch a glimpse of the Matterhorn."

I was grateful for the distraction and raised my head in an effort to see the theme park replica of my favorite peak, but the gurney's straps prevented me from getting a look. Still, having just been to the base of the real thing in Switzerland, I had a crystal clear picture in my mind. It was as though this pilot was instinctively aware of my passion for mountains and my particular recent history with the Matterhorn.

At Good Samaritan Hospital, Craig arrived just as I got situated in a room. Soon after, a mature, gray-haired gentleman with a trustworthy face walked in and introduced himself as Dr. Cannom, a specialist in electrophysiology. He explained what, based on the information he had received, was likely to follow. From his tone of voice, we could tell that this was much bigger and more alarming than we could have ever expected. He patted my knee and said, "You're in good hands, and you'll be fine."

As he departed, there was complete silence. My parents had just arrived from Northern California and no one knew what to say—or worse, what not to say. I felt the heaviness of everyone's fears. That's when I lost it.

"I really don't think I'm going to be fine," I screamed. "There's something going on. I don't think he's being straight with me."

Craig darted from the room in search of the doctor. "Please, Dr. Cannom," he'd pleaded, "you've got to tell me what's really going on here. What do we need to do?" Despite Craig's impassioned request for specifics, the doctor's response remained vague. "We've got a serious problem here," he confirmed, "but we don't know to what extent just yet. First we have to complete some tests." This wasn't good enough for Craig. He hated feeling so powerless, as if watching me being overpowered by a tidal wave and unable to throw me a lifeline.

Returning to my room and taking his place by my hospital bed, he was uncharacteristically quiet. Craig, the man who always knew what to say, found it impossible to utter a word. His emotion-fueled silence only made it worse for me. Convinced he was keeping something from me, my thoughts began to spin out of control, piling one wild worst-case scenario on top of another. Between sobs, I begged for him to open up and tell me what the doctor had said. Instead, my father, a man of very few words, especially in really difficult situations, began to speak.

"Kelly, relax and give Craig a moment," Dad said softly but firmly. "He loves you very much, and is just as scared as you are." The conviction of my father's words calmed me. I realized no one was hiding anything from me—we were all just in a state of shock.

After waiting for the Memorial Day weekend to end and hospital staff to return to full capacity, I was finally taken down to the Electrophysiology Lab for the first of many invasive procedures where my heart would be put through a multitude of rigorous tests. Craig accompanied me to the procedure room, clutching my hand until he was not allowed to go any further. This first and most critical test was the heart biopsy, which indicated I had cell damage from what appeared to be a viral infection. The virus was judged idiopathic, meaning the origin is unknown. My condition was not genetic, nor a result of my lifestyle. Somewhere, sometime within the past few months, I contracted—probably through inhalation—a virus. It could have attacked any part of the body. In my case, it rooted in my heart. It left scar tissue in my left ventricle, short-circuiting my heart rate and causing Ventricular Tachycardia (VT), which manifests as a fast heart rhythm that can be fatal.

We knew I was in for the long haul. It was time to get used to the hospital environment. All the rooms on the floor were private, equipped with high tech telemetry equipment designed to carefully monitor each patient's fragile heart. The otherwise sparse room had a bed, side table, and cubbyhole where I could stow my clothes and personal items. Late one morning my mom mentioned her feet hurt. Since we've always worn the same size, I offered her my shoes, a brand new pair of tennis sneakers. Craig went to the cubbyhole to retrieve the shoes, but couldn't find them. I knew they'd made their way to the hospital, because I had them with me when we arrived. We polled the nurses and staff, but no one had seen them. Craig set out to find them and, eager for something to do, my mom joined him in the search. About fifteen minutes later, they returned without the shoes but were sporting wide grins. It was hard to imagine anything funny about an errant pair of tennis shoes, until they described their visit to the hospital's "lost and found" room. The space was filled with the expected jumble of commonplace items like sweaters and umbrellas. But, much to their surprise and twisted delight, among the unclaimed detritus, abandoned in a corner, was a prosthetic leg. Craig and my mom concocted a zany scenario, imagining some poor, one-legged sole being discharged from the hospital, his wife loading him into the car and saying "Now honey, are you sure you have everything?" It was just the antidote we needed, our accumulated tension melting away as we all fell about laughing. Humor, we'd learned, would prove to be as much a source of healing as any remedy.

Once the electrophysiology test results were viewed and extent of damage was determined, the goal was to find a medication or "cocktail" of combined medications that would control these fast rhythms. Finding the right drugs would be a challenge in and of itself, but the real shocker came when I was told they wanted to implant a relatively new device called an AICD (Automatic Implantable Cardioverter Defibrillator). It was a large, stainless steel appliance of sorts, about the size of a Sony Walkman®, that was to be surgically inserted into my abdomen. Wires leading out of the apparatus would thread up through a vein in my torso, ultimately ending with screws into my heart. If my mind didn't go numb with the image of a box protruding from my flat stomach, I definitely checked out with the thought of someone screwing wires into my heart. Before agreeing to so risky a procedure I needed more information so I could properly process what this cardiac thingamajig was for. The doctor's explanation was that the device was designed as a back up, in case my medications didn't control my arrhythmias. In layman's terms, it was an "in-body" version of a paramedic's paddle.

Recognizing my nervousness, Dr. Cannom brought a sample device into my room to let me see, touch, and feel. At approximately three-inches tall by four-inches wide, and nearly an inch deep, it initially seemed manageable. Until, that is, he placed it on my stomach where it would be implanted. For a large, overweight man, the device would hardly be noticeable. But for me, 110 pounds at best and seemingly losing weight by the minute, the device seemed more like a shoebox. So much for my initial vision of an implant—the device would be a big deal, protruding quite obviously from my stomach. I felt nauseous with the thought of it all, but only for a moment.

My overwhelming fear of my heart racing erratically quickly took over and kept my vanity in check.

I went into surgery. It was my first time, and I was terrified. As a result, my body seemed to reach an all-time adrenaline high, causing me to become stronger than seemed possible. Just prior to the procedure, the anesthesiologist gave me the appropriate sedative dose for my body weight and size. I was out of it for a while. Then, alarmingly, I began to hear the surgeons speaking. I also felt a pulling and tearing sensation in my lower abdomen. I wished so desperately that I could talk and tell them I was awake, but couldn't move. I was immobile, completely paralyzed, and I was "feeling." I feared the force of the pulling would increase, but I could not speak out. There was nothing I could do. I had no movement, no voice. I must have flinched, as suddenly all sensation again fell away. Hours later, I woke up in the recovery room. The anesthesiologist came by to check on me. I told him everything, and he said, "Not possible, we gave you plenty of anesthetic." He continued to doubt me, until I asked him what he was laughing about during the surgery. He was alarmed, and persisted in asking me more details. After discussing my claim with the surgeons, he concluded that I was partially conscience and the tearing sensation was when they stretched the skin in my skinny stomach over the thick device. You can bet that I now make sure the surgeons know I am out, regardless of the "appropriate" dosage. For a person who once disliked drugs, I now can't get enough!

I loved knowing that the implanted AICD offered my heart a "safety net," but was an emotional wreck, constantly waiting for the device to unexpectedly fire. I was in a perpetual state of low-grade panic. Not wanting fear or anxiety to accelerate my heart rate and potentially induce shock, I worked hard to stay calm and curb my emotions. I needed to separate my head from my heart.

By the time I was discharged on October 4, I'd spent a month in the hospital. After a seemingly endless series of failed attempts to identify a tolerable medication, I was prescribed Amiodarone and Lanoxin. They came equipped with a whole new host of problematic side effects, but seemed, as a combination therapy, to adequately suppress my arrhythmias. Released from Good Sam, my eyes welled up with emotion as we reached the coast and I was able to take in the ocean view. My perspective had been forever altered. It was good to be home, but I genuinely felt disabled. Craig began to take me for short strolls along a popular boardwalk in Newport Beach, but after a mere ten or so yards, my body would begin to lose balance, causing me to stumble like a drunken sailor. It must have been quite a sight, and perhaps an embarrassment for Craig. If I could have consciously registered how far from a fit runner I had come, I would have been emotionally crushed. But Craig would allow none of that. He stayed right by my side to reassure me that my symptoms were temporary. This was my hope.

After just one week at home, I began to experience pauses in my heartbeat, accompanied by lightheadedness and hot flashes. Just seven days after leaving the hospital, I was readmitted through the emergency room. One fix was cause for another problem. After four days of adjusting my medications and monitoring my rhythms, it was determined I needed an additional piece of machinery, this time a pacemaker. The AICD would take care of my heart rate on the high end, and the pacemaker would keep it in line at the low end. In just over a month, I would be having another device implanted; I was quickly turning into the Bionic Woman; the difference being that she controlled her super power whereas my built-in power had control over me, and there was nothing "super" about it. On October 15, I went through a surgery that stretched to more than three hours. Normally this is a quick operation, but because the surgeon needed to work around the existing AICD wire already secured in my heart the procedure took much longer than expected, meaning more drugs and a longer recovery period. For days afterward, I couldn't snap out of my postsurgery gloom. The doctors couldn't understand why. The surgery appeared successful. Both mechanical devices were functioning as prescribed and my routine lab results seemed normal. Ever vigilant, Craig suspected something was up when he discovered my white blood count was 5,000, a number the doctors regarded as acceptable. Craig questioned this, insisting they look more closely at *my* numbers, not the normal figures. Ever since I'd initiated drug therapy, my white blood count had dipped down to the 2,500 range, which was my new "normal." Craig voiced his concern to the doctors, suggesting my body was trying to fight something. It wasn't until the next morning when I woke up with a raging fever of 103 degrees, that the doctors finally reacted. Within hours, Craig's fears were confirmed. I had been fighting a life-threatening staph infection at the suture site. I was immediately pumped full of antibiotics, taken to the Nuclear Medicine department for a gallium scan to look for hidden infections, and then wheeled into the operating room for emergency surgery to remove the pacemaker.

After leaving the hospital for the second time, Craig contacted my former primary physician, the doctor with whom I'd first discussed my concerns; the one who'd urged me to see a psychiatrist. Craig was eager to gather as much medical history as possible, hoping it might prove helpful moving forward. The doctor talked nervously and cautiously, feeling guilty, I suspect, about his perceived oversight. After Craig informed him of what had transpired since my last visit, the doctor sheepishly offered the rationale that, "In spite of Kelly's symptoms, she didn't fit the profile of someone who would have a heart condition. I just didn't expect it. It's like, when you hear the sound of hoof steps coming across a wooden bridge, you expect to look up and see a horse. In Kelly's case, it was a zebra."

Though I was blessed with great support, my world was closing in on me, becoming smaller with each passing week. Craig's and my isolation was self-prescribed. We simply didn't have the energy to socialize, knowing it would require us to provide, time and time again, detailed explanations of my medical dramas. Reliving it became more and more exhausting, especially for Craig who didn't want to burden me with the task. As I rested, Craig spent days and nights either tracking my symptoms or dealing with the ceaseless medical bills. While he did a great job as a caretaker, his work suffered. It was futile for him to go into his office. He was distracted, constantly worrying about me while updating concerned and caring coworkers about my health status. We both felt trapped, physically and emotionally hemmed in by my illness.

One long day, after being readmitted yet again to Good Samaritan and after thirty-one continuous hours of VT, I broke down and cried in Craig's arms, fearing my heart would never slow down. I felt I was robbing him of the future we envisioned. I feared the deterioration of my heart may be the beginning of a downward health spiral, and I did not want to take Craig down with me. I also worried about the long-term effect of all the toxic drugs. Since I had been diagnosed, my healthy blood had turned to poison. We had heard, read, and even signed disclosures about the litany of potential diseases, organ damage or failure, as well as constraints recited by the doctors. One reoccurring theme: *pregnancy under your circumstance could be life-threatening . . . do not take this drug if you are pregnant or breast-feeding.* As hearing such words became routine, I grew increasingly despondent. We put aside all discussion of starting a family, and I silently agonized over the threat of losing my youth, our adventurous life, and the prospect of raising children together. I knew Craig felt the same, but it was just too hard to talk about. As if he was reading my mind, he offered a warm hug that brought me back to my trusting safe place. I knew somehow everything would work out. "This is not happening to *you,*" he gently whispered, "it's happening to *us.* We are a team, and we're going to pull through this *together.*"

CHAPTER 3

Shock Therapy

IT was a dramatic year of firsts for me—my first arrhythmia, defibrillator, and pacemaker, plus a stubborn infection and radioactive drugs. And while I miraculously survived it all, there was one thing, perhaps innocuous by comparison, that might have pushed me over the edge: the hospital food. My medical team never put me on a specific diet; I could pick from any of what the hospital considered "nutritious" choices—a steady stream of bland, industrialized food, all of uniform consistency. Most disconcerting was the seemingly lack of attention to the heart-clogging fat that many of the meals contained. Thank God for my wealth of nutrition knowledge. (In college my nickname was "Temple Kelly," owing to my healthy eating habits.) Determined to maintain what strength I had left, I wanted to eat well to get well. It was hardly the time for a vacation from my heart-healthy habits.

Improving hospital fare is an absolute imperative. Many health institutions are stuck in the "Wonder Bread" days, offering foods that *make you grow in twelve different ways*! Most of the patients in my cardiac unit were there for plumbing purposes—to clean out their seriously congested arteries, the very result of poor food choices. Some large urban hospitals even boast a McDonald's franchise!

Hospital food is reminiscent of the notorious candy bowl at the dentist's office, reinforcing poor habits, except the consequences are far more dangerous. It is almost as if the medical system wants to supply its customers with the fix that will bring them right back through its doors.

Though Craig understood and supported my quest for life-preserving nutrition, he often grew frustrated with me. One day, after a particularly challenging hospital stint, he said, "You were just injected with radioactive dye and you are worried about fat in your food?" As he watched my weight drop below one hundred pounds, he would insist, "You need to eat. *Eat anything!*" He was right in that I needed calories; yet, I couldn't bring myself to consume what I perceived as the final nail in my coffin.

Transforming his words of support into action, Craig began making daily excursions in search of the foods I enjoyed most. Eating my deliciously nutritional meals and snacks was as much a boon to my emotional health as it was to my physical well-being, helping me to cope with the dull sameness of my hospital-bound existence.

Craig, my ever-thoughtful Prince Charming, may have thought he was catering to a princess, but more than once this bedridden princess turned into an ogre. Occasionally, when challenged to get something—*anything*—down, I would become ultra-picky and refuse to eat whatever was on offer unless it was precisely right. Craig rolled with my irritating perfectionism. He would simply eat whatever I didn't. He never complained, and rarely stepped out to get anything special for himself. He would even make-believe he liked the food, insisting, "Yum! This is good!" Yet, despite my endless cravings and demands, his loving devotion never dimmed. In fact, the only thing missing from my dinners was candlelight—which is not permitted in the hospital due to the use of oxygen.

One of my nurses commented, "Craig, you are a saint for bringing food in every day for Kelly." Craig sat at the base of my bed and, with typical modesty, responded, "It's the only thing she can control right now. I'm glad to do it."

Deep down, he understood me. But, more than that, he cared and wanted to help in any way he could to get me through the day. Soon, Craig had his own hospital fan club. All the nurses who witnessed his support quickly fell in love with him.

Like food, exercise was one of the few things I could control. While I was very frail, I remained determined to do something, even if it was a walk around the nurses' station supported by an IV pole on one side and Craig on the other. My test was if I could stand, I would walk. I would look at the wall clock, and every few hours do a few laps, all in the hope of maintaining some semblance of strength. The biggest challenge was running into nurses who had returned from several days off. Surprised to see I had not left, they would say, "Are you still here?" I heard this question much too often, further fueling my fear and frustration that the doctors couldn't fix me. Other patients came and went, while my cockamamie heart kept me anchored to a prison of monitors.

By mid-June 1993, I was back home for what I hoped might be an extended stay. But my bubble of hope was burst one sunny afternoon when Craig and I went for a casual bike ride on the strand, a five-mile stretch of land along the perimeter of Newport Beach Peninsula. The flat, concrete path is a chaotic jumble of walkers, bikers, and skaters bordered by a deep sandy white beach that ends at a surf jetty called The Wedge. There are piers, restaurants, the Newport-Balboa Ferry, and boat rentals. Because it's both a popular tourist spot and a local hangout, the area is always buzzing. Initially I felt invigorated by the surrounding energy; but, as the day progressed, I began feeling lightheaded and queasy. I had become so attuned to my body by now that I could gauge my heart rate by my level of fatigue. My heart had begun to race and the rhythm wasn't breaking. I became nervous. My breathing became labored and I found it difficult dealing with the massive crowd of people. We immediately packed up and drove home to call the hospital. The cardiac unit had given me a device that, when placed on my chest, could transmit my heart rhythm over the phone. The transmission would indicate if I were safe, needed to come in or, worse case scenario, call 911. It was already at 140 bpm and I was terrified that it would creep up to the danger zone of 190, which would induce "shock therapy." The doctor at the cardiac unit told us to remain calm and to keep monitoring the rate. Usually, the rhythm would break after a few hours or so, and I'd be fine. Not this time. The fast rhythm had begun to suck up all my energy. I tried to eat dinner, but it made me woozy. My heart was pumping so poorly, I was unable to digest my food. Slumped in a chair, I attempted to remain calm. I knew if I let my fear take over, my heart rate would further escalate. I kept telling myself, "Keep your emotions inside. Hold it all in, Kelly. Don't let your heart know how terrified you are." I actually thought I could trick my heart into a slower rhythm by pretending to remain composed. Craig kept looking at me for some sign that things were easing up, gently prodding, "Kelly, how are you feeling? How's your stomach?"

My whole body seemed off-kilter, and my posture showed it. I tried to cough; hoping the forced contraction would cause a break in the heart rate. Nothing happened. I kept feeling weaker and weaker. I focused on every beat, waiting for my haywire heart's electrical system to short-circuit so that it would return to its steady sinus rhythm. I was imprisoned in a body set on fast forward.

As long as he understood what was going on and felt a sense of control, Craig could maintain unflustered. Even when his sense of calm abated, he was usually able to fake, eager to appear strong for me. But as my situation worsened, he could no longer keep up his guard. He began trembling. "Why are you shaking?" I asked. Trying not to alarm me, he casually brushed it off, responding, "I'm a little cold." In the days and months that followed, whenever the fear and uncertainty became overwhelming, these shivering episodes would recur. My rock was reducing itself to rubble.

Craig could clearly see I was in bad shape. As the hours passed, I withdrew into my own thoughts, putting up a wall between myself and everything else. Somehow it just felt safer to shut out the reality of what was going on. Craig tried a trick he'd learned at the hospital—he cupped his hand and hit me hard on the back in an effort to break the rhythm. He tried this repeatedly, but to no avail. He kept asking if he should call the doctor, but I didn't want him to. Each time he asked, I just shook my head "no." As the hour grew late, I became so exhausted that I just decided to go to bed, hoping—as had happened before—that the rhythm would break during the night. I told Craig, "Let me just sleep it off." Craig carried me upstairs, laid me in bed, and sat vigil as I tried to doze.

In an effort to "read" my heart rate, Craig kept count of my pulse, as if this quantitative information could help him "see" the problem. He was desperate to know if the numbers were going up or down. We were both worried, but neither of us really wanted to make the sixty-mile drive to the hospital. Nor did I want to chance being stuck on the L.A. freeway with a frighteningly fast heart rhythm. I was just as afraid for Craig as for myself, terrified of the thought of him in the driver's seat, one hand on the wheel and the other monitoring my pulse. What if I passed out or went into cardiac arrest?

"Kelly, should I call the doctor?" Craig asked for the umpteenth time, even though he knew I was half-asleep. "No!" I barked, barely lifting my head off the pillow. "Just leave me alone!" I knew I was unfairly lashing out at him, but at that moment all I cared about was losing myself in sleep. Sixteen hours of racing rhythm had taken its toll. I closed my eyes as my head sank into the pillow.

Suddenly, as if from faraway, I heard the panic in Craig's voice. "Kelly, *Kelly*, are you OK? Your heart rate's *really* fast." But I couldn't move or answer him. He had again checked my pulse, which had further increased in rate. It was now a race against time. I was in grave danger.

He saw I was turning a bluish grey and when he touched me, felt that my skin had become icy cold. He shook me hard, but I didn't feel it. I had lost consciousness. In a frantic attempt to rouse me from my stupor, a last ditch effort to revive me, he firmly slapped me across the face. He shouted, "Kelly," and began cursing himself; infuriated he hadn't called the doctor and rushed me to a hospital sooner. He dialed 911, begged for them to send an ambulance as soon as possible, lifted me off the bed and lay me on the floor in preparation to perform CPR. My pulse was light but very fast. Within minutes, he heard the approaching siren and ran down to open the door and direct the paramedics upstairs. They promptly pulled out a pair of sheers, sliced open my negligee and put the electrodes on my chest to get an EKG. In the meantime, Craig passed the phone, with the hospital's on-call specialist on the other end, over to one paramedic while informing another of my medications and medical history. As soon as they grasped what was up, concluding my heart was racing just a few beats under the cutoff rate of 190 which was set as my defibrillator's minimum threshold, they promptly put me on a gurney and carried me down the narrow stairs. By the time we arrived at the front door, my blood pressure had taken a further plunge. One of the paramedics charged the hand paddles and externally defibrillated me. I came to. I was disoriented and felt a burning sensation in my chest. My eyesight was blurry and I couldn't' make out who was with me. The paramedic read my confused look and introduced himself.

"I will be right here to hold your hand," he reassured me. "You are going to be OK." Holding on for dear life, I was loaded into the ambulance and taken to Mission Hospital to be stabilized. Again, Craig followed. I was then transferred by ambulance to Good Sam to see Dr. Cannom. Boluses of drugs, including a sedative to calm me, were administered intravenously. My heart quieted and I was finally able to relax. I asked Craig what had happened. In his usual manner, he made light of the situation as he recalled the evening's rollercoaster ride.

He jokingly said, "Five good looking paramedics gallantly ran up the stairs looking for you and saw you lying on the bed. They nestled in close and tore off your purple silk negligee. " He paused, then added, "And imagine, you slept through the whole thing!"

This episode instigated one of our longest continuous hospital stints—six weeks that seemed never-ending. Soon after I was reinstalled at Good Sam, the doctors discovered it was still too soon to start an experimental drug they had hoped would help. Instead, they chose to implant the next generation of high-tech devices, equipped with ATP (automatic Tachycardia Pacing). It had the capability of pacing with gentler shocks in an effort to break a fast rhythm before delivering the strong shock. As a result, the threshold could be set lower so my body didn't have to endure these fast "resting" rhythm marathons. There was another reason for upgrading the device. My first AICD was an outmoded model. The doctors were not allowed to implant the latest experimental version because the "lead wires" they were using were also experimental. The FDA prohibits the use of two experimental devices at the same time, so the doctors gave me a choice as to which technology I wanted in me. The decision was easy. One required open chest surgery and the other didn't. I was terrified of the image of a permanent "zipper" on my chest. Due to subsequent FDA approval of the experimental lead wires that were already threaded into my heart, I could now take advantage of the leading edge AICD technology. The timing was perfect, and I went into surgery.

Two days afterward, I got my first series of full-strength shocks. I was terrified. The gentler ATP technology was activated but my heart did not respond. My heart became active and I received not just one, but multiple vigorous shocks. After the last of them, I temporarily blacked out. Exhausted from fear, tears rolled down my cheeks. The doctors tried to reassure me they would make adjustments to the settings to keep it from happening again. But the problem wasn't the device; the doctors were challenged to find an effective drug. Because I had already tried and failed most of the medications designed to counteract my symptoms, another experimental drug was proposed. In order to qualify, I was scheduled for an EPS (electrophysiology study), standard protocol before beginning an experimental drug that is still in trials and not yet approved for use. This EPS test would prove that I did, in fact, have a heart condition, thereby providing data for the drug company to submit to the FDA as part of the approval process. In order to gather this information, they needed to take me off all drugs. They were, in a way, inviting my heart to act up, thereby proving my "condition." Result: seven more full-strength shocks.

As timing would have it, my mom was there to see me getting shocked. A nurse caught sight of the color draining from her face, grabbed hold of her, and took her to a small waiting room. She was dizzy and, aiming for a chair, missed the seat and fainted to the floor. Now she, too, was admitted. She was given a sedative and after a couple hours of rest, was released with a prescription of Xanax. My mom experienced everything I did, with twice the intensity. She too had a broken heart. As she lost weight, my dad, who eats during periods of stress, put it on.

During times of chaotic heart behavior, in between the testing of new "pill-form" medications, the doctors would hook me up to an IV of Lidocaine, a "drip" medication that usually provided a period of stabilization. (Since it wasn't available in pill form, I couldn't be discharged on it.) It was a great drug. However, if I stayed on the Lidocaine drip for any significant length of time, the toxicity would build up in my system and cause some unusual side effects. Among them was severe queasiness, augmented by an ill feeling comparable to blind drunkenness with disturbing hallucinations.

My EPS test results and subsequent shocks proved my case, and I immediately began the new experimental drug. But instead of slowing down my rhythms, it did just the opposite, accelerating my heart rate. The drug was immediately discontinued. However, the half-life was eight hours, which meant my heart would be out of control until it was flushed from my system. I tried to hold myself together, praying the gadgetry inside me wouldn't fire.

After three long weeks in the Cardiac Care Unit, I was able to move to a floor for less critical patients, where I tried yet another drug, a drug that would be a real miracle if it worked. It would allow me to decrease my medications from twenty-eight to twelve pills a day. This time, the drug actually showed promise, until around midnight when I broke out into an allergic type reaction. It was torturous—unrelenting, systemic itchiness, like a thousand internal bee stings. I was given more medication—several different kinds to help alleviate the symptoms, but nothing worked. Meanwhile, I scratched myself like crazy. Since the itch was internal, I could gain no relief. Then my body gave up. I started to convulse as if I was having seizures. My nerve impulses were going crazy. Nothing worked to control my spasms. It was unbearable. Craig, every bit as frightened as I was, stayed up all night rubbing my skin obsessively, unsuccessfully trying to distract me from the stings. At one point he screamed at the nurses, yelling, "Do something!" He even went a step further, calling Dr. Cannom at home at 3:00 A.M. to ask for help. Sedatives were administered, and I finally went to sleep at 5:00 A.M. Just as I was starting to feel relief from the sedatives, my heart jumped back into a fast rhythm. It was a relentless cycle that would make the sanest person go mad. It was time to temporarily return to the most effective drug, Amiodarone, which was also the most brutally toxic.

Because I seemed so out of control, unbeknownst to me Craig asked for a private meeting with Dr. Cannom to talk about my future. He didn't feel my mom could emotionally handle much more, but invited my dad to join the discussion.

Meeting with them in a small consultation room a few doors down the hall, Dr. Cannom made the shocking pronouncement that, "at some point and time, Kelly will need a transplant." My dad could not bear hearing this news. He knew little of transplants and did not like the prognosis. His mind shut down in a protective avoidance, and he closed himself off from the rest of the conversation. Craig's reaction was the total opposite; he wanted and needed to know more—everything and anything. My fate was his fate. Finally, Craig bravely pronounced, "If this is what we need, let's do it now before she gets too sick."

Dr. Cannom explained that it wasn't that simple. "The waiting list for hearts is long and the donors are few. Only the most critically ill patients have a chance. Picture it this way. It's as if Kelly is going down a river and ahead lays a waterfall. Our goal is to catch her before she goes over." The instructions were clear, but Craig interjected, asking, "You mean I need to watch for the signs—that point when she's at the edge of heart failure—and of death? It seems so risky." Dr. Cannom reassured them, "This small window is the most opportune time for Kelly to qualify as a priority transplant candidate."

Before Dr. Cannom left the room, they all decided it was best to keep this a secret from me. They feared the added anxiety would only increase my suffering. My dad felt badly for Craig, knowing it would be a double burden to live with so immense a secret and remain on constant watch for the precise right time—that slender moment between near death and new life.

While Craig left the meeting wanting to learn all that he could about transplants, my dad remained in denial. He resorted to what he knew best, his faith, and simply prayed my body would somehow learn to tolerate my symptoms. He couldn't contemplate a transplant. What he truly desired was desperately clear: he wanted to trade places with me.

Illness is very revealing of relationships. Some of our closest friends, and even family members, stayed far away. Others who I expected far less from were eager to help carry the burden, offering unconditional support. But mostly, they would pop by, say nothing, give a hug, share some tears and walk out. Craig tried to keep his emotions in check, determined to stay strong for me. Only rarely would he walk someone out and return with damp eyes. In spite of the comfort I got from his strong façade, it was equally comforting to see him surrender.

Even during periods of stability, the shadow of death always lurked nearby, a constant reminder of just how frail life is, even with the best of care. During one hospital stay I was assigned one of two "Jack and Jill" rooms, sharing a common bathroom. The man in the adjoining room coded: massive heart attack. Although emergencies are expected in a hospital, it's daunting to be on the sidelines hearing a team of doctors and nurses work on someone, vigorously administering CPR and then, suddenly, a deadly silence.

During extended hospital stays, Craig and I sought any and every ounce of normalcy. One night, I put Craig up to an unusual challenge—a romantic tryst in my hospital bed. Hey, I wasn't dead yet! During the day, the doctors had put me back on Lidocaine to stabilize my heart while trying to identify a new medication. On this particular occasion, I was feeling "high," more specifically, frisky. As midnight was approaching, I'd been on the drip most of the day and the intensity of my desire began to rapidly escalate. I needed to be with Craig as desperately as I needed my next breath. Ever since my first hospital visit, my sexual appetite had all but disappeared. So, Craig was more than willing to accommodate my unexpected arousal. Still, I was hooked up to a drip IV and had multiple wires connecting me to a heart rate monitor—not exactly the standard paraphernalia for a romantic interlude.

No worries! Craig, being the supportive guy he is, was happy to oblige. Problem was, he didn't want me to go into a fast or unsafe rhythm. So, he decided to delicately explain the situation to one of the nurses. Her job was to view the heart rate monitors from the nurses' station, reporting and addressing any unusually rapid patterns. If, of course, Craig was, shall we say at the top of his game, the beats should be very rapid; but the rapid beats would signal the alarms and alert the nurses, who would be duty-bound to interrupt. Faced with so unusual a request, she decided it was necessary to consult the head nurse. Knowing we were a young couple who had been cooped up in a hospital for some time, the head nurse was sympathetic to our request. However, she too was concerned over the potential for problem rhythms, so decided it was necessary to contact the on-call doctor. As our request traveled up the chain of hospital command, I was becoming more and more anxious, as was Craig, who worried my intense desire would abate. Finally, a nod of approval was received from on high.

The door, adorned with a strict "do not disturb" notice, closed behind us. An audience gathered around the monitor outside.

With Craig and I poised for action, he said he felt like he was walking onto a stage. In a way, he was. A good performance could bring an army of doctors and nurses rushing in to save my life. A bad performance, and Craig would be the one dying that night. The pressure was intense. We started off slowly, exercising extreme caution.

Craig keeping a close eye on the heart rate monitor above the bed. Naturally, as things started to heat up, so did my heart.

The next morning, there were two delightful developments. First, Dr. Cannom didn't stop by for his routine visit. Later, we realized that the "do not disturb" sign was still up and, embarrassingly enough, the kindly doctor had been fully briefed about our midnight tryst.

Second, everyone treated Craig like a superstar.

After three months of on-and-off hospital time, we reached the critical one-year mark. Craig and I went to see Dr. Cannom to evaluate my most recent tests and learn if there had been any improvement in my status. The news wasn't good. When he sighed and said, "There has not been any change in your heart," I felt like I'd been submerged underwater, sinking fast. I was so blindly hopeful, so utterly convinced that my heart would show improvement, that I wasn't prepared for any other scenario. Dr. Cannom could tell what a fragile state I was in. As he reviewed my chart, he put a positive spin on the results. "Your heart function is currently at 35 percent [I knew 60 percent was normal]." When he smiled and gently added, "Hopefully, over the next year things are going to get better." I wanted, indeed *needed*, more than anything to embrace his note of optimism, however cautious it might have been.

Doctor Cannom encouraged us to maintain as normal a schedule as possible. Considering my chest full of electrified implants and the drug-induced fog I spent much of my time lost in, "normal" had become a relative term. Constantly aware of my limitations, our activities generally consisted of easy walks and, on a few occasions, a bike ride. Craig was game to go whenever wherever, and took full advantage of even the smallest windows of opportunity. Even on good days, we kept to the flatlands, heading for the beach, Balboa Island or Dana Point Harbor. Our first priority was always to share at least a modicum of physical activity. Exercise had always been my lifeline, and I was determined to hold onto it. Then, if I were feeling up to it, we'd add on small treats—lunch, or maybe even a modest dinner. But dinner dates were rare because, by the time evening rolled around I'd taken my full day's fix of medication. Embalmed by my pharmaceutical cocktail, I was hardly what you'd call a sparkling dining companion.

Since my heart was pumping insufficient blood to my extremities, I was always cold. As springtime blossomed in Southern California, everyone else was running around in tank tops and shorts, while I sat bundled in layers of winter clothes, trying to ward off purple fingers and toes. Physical exertion enhanced my circulation. More important, it helped rid my body of rapidly accumulating toxins. Moving old drugs through my system before adding more always made me feel better.

Though Craig's physical strength and stamina were as impressive as ever, to help boost my motivation, he slowed his pace. I would often ask, "How am I doing? Am I slow today?" Unbeknownst to me, he would shorten his stride to make sure his foot landed a few inches behind mine. It was his quietly generous way of giving me a psychological advantage, letting me believe I wasn't losing ground. Such seeming triumphs, tiny as they were, proved enormously therapeutic. On bad days—days when my downward physical spiral seemed inevitable—I could recall these little victories and use them to spin a more positive attitude.

Craig was constantly figuring out subtle ways to boost my spirits, and once concocted a delightfully clever way to do the same for my parents. When mom and dad called to say they were headed south for one of their regular visits, Craig, the consummate prankster, decided to play a harmless joke on them. Prior to their arrival, he used our VCR to record two episodes of *Jeopardy*. He then viewed the tapes and compiled separate lists of each episode's answers and questions. Soon after my parents arrived, we all gathered around the TV to relax. Without either of them noticing, Craig activated the tape just as the real show was scheduled to air. Lounging nonchalantly on the couch with a magazine in his lap, his secret sheet of answers nestled between the pages; he pretended to be only mildly engaged in what was happening on screen. Then, as the categories were presented, he began to casually toss off correct answers to each question. At first, my dad who prides himself on being a trivia buff, figured Craig had simply hit a lucky streak. By halfway through the first round, dad started to sit up and take notice. Upon Craig's flawless completion of the first round, both mom and dad said how amazed they were. Being in on the joke, I chimed in to say he was always like this. Craig's perfect game continued straight through both the second and "final *Jeopardy*" rounds. They were utterly shocked. This was years before headline grabbing mega-champ Ken Jennings, and they'd never seen anyone come close to getting every single question right. They knew Craig was sharp, as demonstrated by his remarkable retention of medical facts and figures relating to my illness, but they had no idea he was this bright. The following night, Craig gave a repeat performance. My parents' heads were spinning. They were so proud, thrilled to discover his true level of genius!

Craig and I were barely able to contain our laughter, but didn't want to burst their bubble straight away. In fact, it was nearly a year later before we sat them down and said, "We have something important to tell you." At first, of course, they assumed it was something medical. Both were relieved, and more than a bit embarrassed, to learn the truth of our *Jeopardy* hoax.

In addition to finding endlessly creative ways to build me up, Craig also crafted a method of preparing me emotionally for my anticipated fate. He devised a process to steadily coerce me out of my fear. Knowing how stubborn I can be, and how I always want what I can't have, he'd say, "You can't possibly qualify for a heart transplant, you're not that sick," or "You'll never get a heart transplant—your heart's too good, you don't meet the eligibility requirements." At first, I would wholeheartedly agree with him. Then, refusing to dwell on the terrifying thought of a transplant, I'd immediately add, "I don't want to talk about it." But as time went on, I started questioning why I wouldn't or couldn't qualify, then began insisting I could and *would* qualify. Craig knew that by getting the topic out in the open, subtly bringing it up again and again, he'd force me to consider it and ultimately desire the one thing that could save my life. The greatest thing about a soul mate is that they often know you better than you know yourself. In due course, his benevolent scheming would literally prove a lifesaver.

The mind is a wonderful thing. I became a master at grasping the good days and erasing the bad ones. Some days, I would sleep as much eighteen hours. But whenever I was awake, I was seldom without company, with Craig or my mom, or both, always by my side. On one of the few occasions I found myself awake and alone, I took a moment to look at my body. Though I'd viewed my many scars and was well aware I'd lost weight from frequent bouts of nausea and poor appetite, I hadn't really *seen* my body in full until that day. Undressing tentatively, I took a deep breath and faced the mirror. In addition to the protruding Walkman-like AICD device in my abdomen, I had incisions on both sides of my clavicle and a six-inch, horizontal scar just above my belly button. Between the scars, I could see a narrow lead wire and every single jutting rib. The figure in the mirror was sobering. I realized my mental image was a far cry from reality. I was pasty white, with sagging skin, protruding bones and jutting machinery. I looked like a neglected plant, desperate for water and sunlight. The image I saw was so upsetting it took my breath away. I suddenly became weak at the knees and had to steady myself on the edge of the bathroom sink. Taking a long, hard look at my body brought me right back in line with reality.

To stay strong, I decided it best to revert to my original way of thinking. I would compartmentalize my body, thinking of it as just organs and tissues—nothing more, nothing less. I'd long since abandoned any sense of modesty. I had been probed and examined by a continuous parade of interns, residents, attending physicians and surgeons. I needed to do what they did and separate the components that comprised my physiology from the person I truly was. I knew it was the only way for me to survive emotionally. Yes, I decided, I could handle any troublesome body issues, even cover them up, but what I couldn't hide was my face. It was so thin, my eyes perpetually dilated, and I had developed deep wrinkles that made me look twice my age. These weren't the sort of creases that, like a roadmap of a life well lived, add character to an aging face. They were the by-product of complete and utter torment. My forehead was grooved, my brow furrowed, and saddest of all, my smile was broken.

Going for walks was my greatest pleasure. Mom, too, loves to get out into the fresh air, so we scheduled a short walk every day when she was in town. On one occasion, I was feeling particularly good, and told my mom I wanted to take the long route back, following a trail that borders the naturally spacious corridor near our home. Mom was thrilled I was feeling so strong, and led the way along a path that, once committed to, offered no short-cuts. Craig, at home working, noticed how long we had been gone and grew concerned. No longer able to focus on what he was doing, he jumped into his jeep and began searching for us. He roamed all the paved streets in the area and came up empty. Realizing there was only one other way to go, he negotiated his jeep along the narrow walking/bike path that was closed off to vehicles. Just as he was nearing the end of the loop, he spotted us. Angry as he was, relief immediately filled his face. Nothing, not even a neighborhood stroll, was easy for us any-more. Waves of fear seemed to underlay everything.

In late 1993, TJ called to share a wonderful piece of news. "I'm pregnant!" she gleefully announced. Though her tone of voice revealed how thrilled she was, she tried to temper her excitement, sensing it might stir up some difficult emotions in me. She knew me much too well. TJ is as close to a sister as a friend can be. I forced myself to sound happy, trying hard to be sincere, but deep down I struggled. I had other friends with kids, but none as close to me as TJ. She'd had Taylor, a beautiful little girl, two years earlier. Back then, I still held out hope that I, too, would someday have the same opportunity. Now things were different. With each passing day, hope was slipping away, and her news hit me unexpectedly hard. I couldn't get out of my head how far my condition had caused Craig and I to drift from our treasured life plan.

We had talked about having a family even before we got married and even picked out a name for a girl, Kendra. Kendra was a cute, wholesome little waitress who, years earlier, had served us at a romantic, wild game fondue place, appropriately named The Grizzly House, in the Canadian ski resort of Banff, Alberta. In envisioning what our combined DNA might result in, Craig and I kept sweet, adorable Kendra in mind. According to our long-prescribed game plan, I should have been doing what TJ was doing, preparing to invite a new life into the world. Instead, I was signing consent forms and directives in preparation for possible death. Though envy ate away at me and plagued me with guilt, deep down I couldn't have been happier for my dear friend. In May of that following year, Casey, our goddaughter, was born!

Not long after Casey's spring arrival, TJ and her husband Jeff planned a weekend visit to her parent's vacation home in Palm Desert, and invited us to join them. It was a short trip and I was feeling fairly stable, so we gladly accepted. They were bringing their bikes, so we decided to do likewise, strapping them to a newly purchased roof rack atop our Jeep Cherokee. After a two-hour drive filled with lively conversation centered round our delight at the prospect of getting away, we arrived in La Quinta. As we pulled up to the community's gated entrance, we remained too engrossed in our conversation to notice the height of the overhang. As the bikes came crashing down on the side of the car we just looked at each other and uttered the five words that had become our shared mantra, "Well, it could be worse."

And, since life is an ongoing learning experience, upon returning home, we repeated the same mistake as we drove into our garage. Once again the bikes came crashing down, this time taking a few pieces of our house along with them. Having grown used to far more dire situations, again we nodded, "well, it could have been worse." But our lesson still wasn't complete. Several weeks later we managed yet another collision between bikes and garage. Finally, we wised up and got a "roof reminder" for the Jeep, accepting that we would likely remain too preoccupied with more pressing issues to worry about than bent bike frames or twisted eaves. Indeed, we knew, it could be worse!

In good times and bad, my heart remained center stage. In January 1994, Craig suddenly woke me in the middle of the night and said, "Don't be afraid, and just follow me." He pulled me under the doorframe, and said, "We're having an earthquake." I swear he's blessed with a caninelike ability to sense these things. Sure enough, moments later it violently hit, shook, and rolled, seemingly without end. Craig was worried the quake would set my nerves jangling, which in turn could increase my heart rate and cause me to get shocked. He feared my elevated heart rate would rival the 6.7 Richter scale measurement of the Northridge Earthquake. It was an extreme example of how we'd become accustomed to taking everything in our lives "to heart," adding elevated tension to even life's scariest moments.

Just as some couples, by rote, climb into their car and commute to work, we'd grown used to dropping everything and driving ninety minutes or more to L.A. to see the doctor or be admitted to the hospital. We always kept a bag packed and waiting by the door, and Craig would lug along his antiquated twenty-five-pound Macintosh computer, the cumbersome precursor to today's featherweight laptops, enabling him to keep working no matter how long our stay turned out to be. I felt so lucky to have him along, not just for safety's sake, but also for his inimitably warm and comforting company. During one particularly long hospital visit, on a day when my heart had been somewhat stable and I was awaiting the next plan of treatment, Craig decided to make one of his few quick trips home to collect the mail and catch up on personal business. Since I had been in the hospital for quite some time, I was feeling low, and the walls were beginning to close in on me. Much to my surprise, Anna and Kris—Dr. Cannom's right-hand nurses—were perceptive to my sullen mood and had come up with a delightful remedy.

Kris came into my room holding a set of nurse's scrubs. She gently threw them on top of my bed and said, "Here, get dressed." I was perplexed, but obliged. Then, Anna came over and started removing my external lead wires from the heart rate monitor. "Okay," Kris trumpeted, "let's get out of here!"

We were all giggling as we made our way down the elevators and through the lobby, my patient ID carefully concealed. Hands linked, we marched out of the hospital and across the street to a nearby café. We sat outside, ordered lunch and enjoyed the fresh air as we shared lighthearted comments about cute doctors, their romantic attachments and other gossipy girl talk. It was the ideal, sunlit tonic for a potentially dark, dreary day. An hour later we returned to the hospital and they hooked me back up to the monitors. By the time Craig returned, all was quiet. When the doctor found out about our cheeky little adventure, he just shook his head and smiled!

CHAPTER 4

Washout

IN an average lifetime, a heart beats approximately two billion times. At thirty-four years old, with all my fast rhythms, I was rapidly depleting my allotted beats. Constantly exhausted, I was becoming less and less able to physically tolerate the relentless weakening of my heart. Simple tasks like going to the toilet could send me into an arrhythmia. My heart was increasingly erratic. When I was in a fast rhythm, I tried everything to control it—meditation tapes, cold showers, laughing, crying, walking, holding my breath—but my heart had a mind of its own. Trying to "control" my heart, I had to monitor not only every physical action but every emotion as well. I clung to the moments when my strength seemed to return a little, rare days when the simplest chore didn't feel like a monumental one.

Increasingly, the insidious symptoms of heart failure began to show. A flight of stairs became as challenging as the last mile up Everest. Often, Craig had to carry me up to bed at night. Knowing that other young women would consider getting scooped up in their attentive lover's arms and carried off to bed a cuddly prelude to a romantic rendezvous only added insult to my injured heart. As Craig carried me, the thought kept running through my head, "Here I am—I once climbed mountains, and now I can't even make it up my own stairs."

I had been on sick leave from work for nearly three years, and it was clear I wasn't going back any time soon. But taking an indefinite leave of absence was a big step. I had grown emotionally dependent on Craig, medically dependent on doctors and devices, and now, no longer contributing to our nest egg, I would be financially dependent. I felt a deep loss of "self." Further depleting was the looming reality forcing me to embrace a brutal truth: my heart was dying. Fortunately, my employer was a large company, Bank of America. I had a compassionate boss who was supported by equally understanding people all the way through to upper management. In 1995, I plucked up the courage to place the call, and then promptly put that corporate chapter of my life behind me in preparation for what now seemed the inevitable. No longer willing to live an increasingly curtailed and claustrophobic life, I finally opened my mind to the possibility of a heart transplant.

I desperately wanted to surround myself with healthy people, not always an easy task when a hospital becomes your home away from home. Still, Craig and I did what we could to help keep faith's fire burning. We spent so much of our time battling powerful physical demons that we needed to restore our souls.

We all had our own methods for keeping our spirits high. Craig brought me inspirational books that he read to me whenever I was feeling sick or needed a distraction. He and dad developed other ways to cope. They often visited the chapel on the hospital's ground floor. Mom prayed, too, but she felt best just being by my side. Making my struggle her own, she revealed a beautiful, caring side. Ever since childhood, I'd been aware of her nurturing skills, but my illness caused them to reach untold depth. Unfortunately, her determination to stand tall on my behalf often resulted in her falling down. She fainted with alarming regularity.

Preparing for the distinct possibility of death, I told Craig I wanted us to be buried beside one another. Even if he remarried, he would still have to end up with me. Making light of my request, he laughed and said, "as if I hadn't been punished enough?" It wasn't the sort of comment I'd come to expect from Craig. Since day one of my illness, he'd sustained an upbeat attitude, constantly expressing his confidence that we were going to get through this. My illness, he insisted, simply represented a hiccup in our life together. Once we emerged from this short, dark tunnel, we'd find ourselves basking in an incredibly bright future. Holding firm to this belief, he grew determined to do everything in his power to convince me and make it a reality. Witnessing the sadness and pity that surrounded us only strengthened his resolve to devise a plan that would ensure our happiness. As my illness progressed, he spent exhaustive hours researching each new medical wrinkle, educating himself on how to combat the problem. Taking care of Kelly was his sole mission.

Family and friends expressed concern to me over Craig's unwavering dedication, noting he needed to carve out time for himself. No one, not even as superhuman a hero as Craig, could keep up so rigorous a caregiving schedule without suffering some emotional side effects, but he refused to acknowledge any personal distress.

It wasn't until I began writing this book, nearly fifteen years after my original diagnosis, that Craig revealed the truth. I was blown away. His obsessive, selfless attentiveness had taken him to the end of a dark path. Preparing for the worst possible outcome, he found himself on a hilltop near my parent's home, overlooking the Queen of Heaven Cemetery. Surveying the rolling green landscape, overlooking a quaint Northern California town, he was impressed with the abundance of fresh flowers accompanying each tombstone. It was so peaceful, so far removed from our turbulent life. He concluded the beautifully maintained grounds would make for a suitable resting place.

Proceeding to the main facility, he sought out the representative who made family arrangements. To fulfill my wish, he wanted to secure a plot for the two of us. In spite of the balmy weather, the building was cold inside. There was a lone desk with a scattering of brochures, which he began to thumb through while waiting for someone to arrive. A well-dressed man finally showed up, looking at young, robust Craig as though he lost his way while visiting an interred relative. He introduced himself, politely asking if he could be of help. Craig didn't know where to begin. He tried to explain, "My wife is sick, and I wanted to do something nice for her. I mean I wanted to take care of her, I mean I . . . I . . . I'm not sure what I mean. . . . Her heart is failing and I am uncertain of our future." The well-dressed gentleman softly asked Craig how he was holding up. Craig was silent. He'd grown used to hearing this question from family and friends but, for some reason, this time it really made him pause and think. Alone with a sympathetic stranger, it was the perfect opportunity to vent, to unload, and to tell someone how crappy our life had become. Standing inside that dim, icy room, Craig began to question his purpose for being there. All the research he'd done to educate himself on my illness was in anticipation of a brighter future. He was always preparing us for better times, a better life. This place was morbid. There was no life.

The representative asked Craig if he would like to sit down. He thought about it, and then said "No. No thank you. I am not supposed to be here. We're not supposed to be here. This is not part of the plan. Not today anyhow. Thank you for your time."

That was it. He had hit his low, pushed off the bottom with both feet, and was on his way back to the surface. He never revealed any of this to me during our struggles because he didn't want me to misinterpret his intentions. He was a planner, yes, but with goals that had a positive motive. The cemetery visit was a departure from the road he wanted us to travel. But courting death forced him to bolster his resolve. More than ever, he wanted us to live.

Craig and my dad both found themselves trying to reach beyond the physical realm, searching for a creative way to get God's attention. Dad adopted a ritual from his devoutly Catholic mom. She claimed she would regularly seek out a new church, one she had never been to before, go to the last pew, kneel, and recite a "Hail Mary." My grandmother lived her last seventy-five of her ninety-two years in the one-church town of Tracy, California; so I'm not sure where, or how, she made such pilgrimages. Still, without question, Dad accepted her theory as if it was doctrine.

Craig's spiritual quest involved the lighting of church candles. In most Catholic churches you can find a sea of votive candles, typically placed inside a large square in front of a statue, stained glass window or other piece of iconography. The parishioner makes an offering by dropping a few coins into the adjoining donation box, then lights a candle and makes an accompanying prayer. Craig's theory was if he lit the candles at all four corners, the dancing flames would surround me with safety. If one of the corner candles were already lit, he'd diligently set about rearranging the tray, adding a fresh candle to complete his protective periphery, all the while being careful not to extinguish any of the existing flames.

I could see that these little journeys provided both of them with a sense of purpose and comfort, and also knew the roads they traveled were, quite literally, littered with peril. Good Sam is in a rather seedy area near Downtown L.A., not the safest or most desirable area to be traipsing from church to church to church. Yet, regularly they would endure the worst the city had to offer in pursuit of their spiritual goals, returning with empty pockets (from distributing it to the needy and spending it on candlelight, not, thankfully, because they'd been mugged!) and hearts filled with colorful tales of their adventures, stories that never failed to distract and delight me.

During this difficult time, staying upbeat meant everything to me, though I sometimes had to reach deep within myself to tap any small measure of hope. As perverse as it may sound, I drew comfort from knowing that several members of my family struggled to overcome some form of drug or alcohol addiction. Knowing people with similar DNA had come through their trials by fire unscathed made it easier for me to believe that I, too, could make it through. I held onto the belief that our family gene pool was lined with tremendous resilience.

Still, I kept hoping for a miracle. One day in the hospital, I turned to my dad and told him that the prayers I had memorized from all my childhood Sunday masses seemed empty. I began feeling guilty that I had so little connection to something deeply spiritual, and I wished I had paid more attention to what the priest had said when I was younger. I had my excuses and, in my defense, it was tough! Weekend masses in a mountain resort make for strange pew mates. In winter, skiers would try to remain inconspicuous as they clunked up the aisle in their heavy boots. Come summer, half the congregation would arrive in skimpy, sometimes barely lawful, beach attire. No matter the season, the colorful parade of tourists proved much more interesting to me than what was happening on the altar. Week after week, I found myself simply showing up and going through the motions: genuflect, stand, sit, pretend to listen and mouth the words to the selected hymns.

Naturally, when the time came to, almost literally, lift up my heart to God, I felt like a hypocrite. Though I'd never before been in such extreme need of divine intervention, I didn't consider myself worthy of asking for God's help. A quote from the Dali Lama leapt to mind: "A tree with strong roots can withstand the most violent storm, but the tree can't grow roots just as the storm appears on the horizon." I felt rootless and, as a result, was driven to look outside myself, to drugs and doctors, for help. I also looked to Craig and dad, whose roots were strong, relying on them to say prayers on my behalf.

In the fall of 1995, my health stabilized long enough for Craig and I to share a trip to the East Coast to see the vivid colors of the changing trees. We charted a driving tour of New England, stopping off in Boston, Nantucket, Kennebunkport, and Newport, Rhode Island. There, we found a beautiful coastline trail that meandered behind the peninsula's stately, historic mansions. Invigorated by the scenery and the cool air, we began to hike along the water. But it wasn't long before I started to feel weak, and Craig had to carry me the last half-mile, before running on to get our car. Yet again, his reserved strength, the result of Craig pacing himself to preserve the illusion of my keeping up, proved a lifesaver.

It was during our New England trip that Craig first noticed a strange sound; a kind of gurgling that accompanied my breathing at night. As always, he'd been engaged in clandestine research about my condition, and recognized the sound as an early indication of congestive heart failure. We barely made it home. While waiting in the L.A. terminal for a connecting flight to Orange County, my heart rate increased and my blood pressure dropped, nausea kicked in and, to avoid fainting, I scrambled to a bench to run through my usual drill—feet up, head down, breathe! Craig followed close behind, pulling out the blood pressure machine while trying to measure my heart rate. I hoped I would regain my composure before paramedics showed up, knowing their appearance would send my stress level soaring. I despised such embarrassing incidents, hating to be at the center of a public scene. I hoped passersby would say a quick prayer for me and move on, thereby helping to alleviate the congestion I was creating, and felt stricken with guilt that someone might miss their flight on account of my foolish heart.

As time passed, I regained blood to my head, color in my face, and began feeling relatively better. A few hours later, our connecting flight having long since departed, Craig arranged for ground transportation to get us home. We remained optimistic that my heart's fast rhythm would break. But, as my body grew steadily weaker, it looked like history would again repeat itself. There was no need to unpack. I was told it was likely my meds were no longer effectively suppressing my temperamental arrhythmias. As a result, my weakened heart was probably causing fluid backup in my liver and lungs. This stagnation would, in turn, further cause my medications to build up to a toxic level, as they were not being flushed out of my system. Bottom line: I needed to be readmitted to the hospital until a new drug therapy could be identified. Only later did Craig tell me that, as he was closing the door of our home, a shuddering premonition stirred deep inside him. I would not, he sensed, be coming home with the same heart.

I felt medically prostituted. I couldn't believe yet another drug was going to be trotted out for me to try. To add further insult, the drug was experimental, awaiting FDA approval. So, for me to qualify for the medication, the doctors needed to do another "washout," a protocol that involved taking me off all my toxic anti-arrhythmia drugs and performing an electrophysiology study. Yes, once again, the drug company needed current data to prove to the FDA that I had a heart condition! As we all anticipated, midway through the washout, my heart went chaotic, switching erratically from a slow rhythm to messy beats, then escalating in rhythm: 130 bpm . . . 140 bpm . . . 150 bpm . . . I failed miserably. I could not be weaned off long enough to try this new wonder drug. I wasn't just disappointed, but also bone-tired. It had become painfully clear to me that my only hope was a transplant.

During this nightmare, my heart's status was reassessed. Things had progressed from bad to worse to all but hopeless. All four of my cardiac chambers, especially the left ventricle, were dilated. My ejection fraction had dropped below 15 percent. With my heart's pumping action compromised, blood pooled in the chambers. This caused further dilation, stretching the valves and walls. What was once a strong muscle had degenerated into a swollen piece of flesh. If that wasn't terrifying enough, it was now threatening to take my good organs with it. I knew my fate was sealed, and told Dr. Cannom, who had become a good friend, so. I think it was as painful for him to hear me acknowledge the inevitable as it was for me to finally accept it.

As much as I was ready to take the next step, my fear didn't dissipate. My thoughts were invaded with images of the physical wound itself, that violent-looking reminder of the surgery: cut skin, open chest, saw through the sternum, pull back the rib cage, cut and uproot my heart. It was hard to let go, knowing I would never again be 100 percent whole. My birth heart would be gone, disposed of in an incinerator as biological/hazardous *waste*. After thirty-four dutiful years, it would simply be tossed aside, taken out with the trash. Still, as Dr. Cannom approached, I offered him a cautious smile, determined to appear positive, even if I had to pretend. He leaned over my bed and, each word weighted with heartfelt regret, quietly stated, "It's time to put you on the list."

CHAPTER 5

"See You Later"

A FTER years of tricky emotional stickhandling, Craig could finally breathe freely, knowing I had embraced my fate. His sensitive way of easing me from ambivalence to acceptance of a transplant had worked. The next hurdle: telling mom and dad. Understandably, they dreaded the word "transplant" as much as me. I was particularly apprehensive about my mom's reaction. On several previous occasions when the word had arisen, she'd fainted dead away. So, when the moment of truth came, I chickened out. Craig took over, stating simply that, "We spoke to Dr. Cannom and Kelly is ready for a transplant. We are okay, and now things will get better." They were actually relieved. Knowing I was better off fighting to stay alive than struggling not to die, we all hugged, wiped our teary eyes and prayed.

None of us knew what to expect with the transplant process. Or at least, that's what I thought. I learned several years later, after picking up a newspaper article, that Craig had done some homework. The article was about a heart and lung transplant patient, named Bill, who had died. What shocked me most was seeing a quote from Craig, who had stood up and said a few words during the memorial service. I was baffled. I questioned, how could this be? Apparently, Craig had followed Bill's 1993 surgery and recovery, as chronicled in the *Los Angeles Times*, and had since befriended he and his wife Bonnie after meeting them at a transplant support group gathering at Hoag Hospital in Newport Beach. At the time, his alibi to me was that he was going to the meeting to educate the members on how to put together a medical records notebook. He had compiled one for me as a way of keeping all the data about my condition in one place, and, to help others do the same, had subsequently self-published *The Personal Health Care Organizer.* Truth be told, he had no intention of talking about the book that night, but instead attended to learn more about life after a transplant. What he heard wasn't entirely comforting. Most of the people, he later recalled, were griping about a whole host of symptoms. Bill and Bonnie proved a cheery, optimistic exception, with Bill delightedly regaling Craig with tales of a post-transplant highlight: a family trip to Disneyland. Sadly, in 1997 Bill went into rejection and died.

I am glad I didn't know about Craig's covert activities during that period, but at least he was armed with some knowledge about what we might expect. Before the doctor could transfer me from Good Sam to UCLA hospital to wait for a transplant, my heart took a turn for the worse and began to deteriorate. It simply wasn't pumping enough blood for the rest of my body. At one critical point, I went into a faster rhythm, my blood pressure dropped and all my vital signs began to fail. Craig and dad were returning from the hospital chapel and, as they neared the CCU, my mom ran toward them calling out, "Kelly is in trouble." They all ran to the room and saw the doctors' frantically working on me. Immediately, a nurse came over and ushered them out, directing them to wait in the hall until they got my vitals under control. The three of them stood there in silence, minutes passing like hours as they anxiously waited to hear something—anything. Just then, TJ called the nurses station and Craig was paged. He picked up the phone and tried to talk, but could not find words. TJ kept asking, "What is going on?" but Craig remained too choked up to speak. She told Craig to catch his breath, then asked, "Is she okay?" After what must have seemed an eternity, Craig bleated a weak, unconvincing "yes."

Craig, the glue holding my parents and I together, was crumbling. TJ knew it was time for her to jump in and help. She immediately made arrangements to fly down from San Francisco and support Craig's caretaker role. TJ would prove the perfect medicine for all of us.

Because of the washout, I now had no therapeutic levels of medication in my system to control my heart. This erratic behavior caused my blood pressure to drop, prompting the doctors to insert a swan ganz (a catheter used for continuous monitoring and pacing of the heart) through the carotid artery in my neck to manually pace my heart back into sinus rhythm. While this procedure worked, the resulting blood pressure level kept me too unstable to be transferred. The ambulance was cancelled. After regaining consciousness, I felt like a runner who was inches from completing a grueling marathon, only to be disqualified. As I faded in and out of consciousness, dad was doing double duty: my mom suffered an emotional breakdown and ended up in the room next to mine.

As the hours slowly ticked past and evening approached, I remained in critical condition, everyone hoping and praying for me to become stable enough to be moved to UCLA. After the major commotion settled, it was once again Craig and I alone with the beeping monitors. We were both numb, exhausted. Having only missed the first night in the hospital with me, Craig requested a cot so he could stay by my side, but it never came. Around midnight, he somehow managed to wedge his tall body into the window frame, dozing in and out with one eye on the monitors as they flashed and beeped. I knew Craig was as terrified as I was, but from his perch on the windowsill he gave me a reassuring smile that let me know everything was going to be all right. His unwavering strength gave me the courage to face what lay ahead. If he were stubborn enough to believe only in the best-case scenario, then I would be, too.

The next morning, Dr. Cannom reviewed my vitals and felt comfortable enough to decide, "Well, it's about as good as it gets. Let's get you out of here." I arrived at UCLA by ambulance and was immediately admitted to the Cardiac Care Unit. It was daunting to see what I was up against. The ten beds in the unit were full, all critical heart patients, most of them seemingly waiting for the same thing, a new heart. The nagging question we all shared, "Would I make the cut?" What was most unnerving was the realization that we were all waiting for a human being to die. A new heart was not something you could pick off the shelf. Simply stated, I would get a heart, if—and *only* if—I was lucky enough. My history with every past treatment had been a question of brand, type, and reliability—whatever suited me best. But, in this case, my heart would not be specially selected for me. It didn't matter if the donor was black, white, male, female, younger, or older. Outside of matching blood, tissue, and size, it was all down to fate. When the first heart transplant was performed in 1967, Dr. Christiaan Barnard said, "For me, the heart has always been an organ without any mystique attached to it . . . merely a primitive pump." Cutting through all barriers, it is about humanity at its most organic level.

I found great strength in redirecting my thoughts to Craig and my parents, focusing on the unstinting love and support they provided. Craig, especially, was phenomenal in his limitless dedication and selflessness. After more than three years of living in the medical world, it was enough to test any marriage. Instead, it brought us closer together. As far as Craig was concerned, nothing ever happened to me. Everything happened to *us*. He stood by my side through everything, big or small. If I was going through it, so was he. He also taught me to be a good sport, encouraging me to rise to every new challenge and find the bright side, even when it seemed all but impossible to see. And he helped me learn to focus on the future, rather than become rutted in the moment. TJ was right when she said, "If you two weren't meant to go through this together, then there is no God, no heaven, and no such thing as unconditional love." For Craig as much as for myself, I had to put up my best fight ever.

Lying in a new bed and in a new hospital hit me hard. It struck me as odd when people told me how brave I was being. After all, it's not like I could jump up and run away! Despite my previous struggle with my faith, a strange thing happened as I prepared myself for what was to come. I simply let go. For the first time in a long, long while, my mind felt at peace. At long last, I had a sense of what it meant to feel as if God was with me, holding my hand. I became filled with a gentle strength I'd never known before. It was as if I had a new sense of freedom, a clear passage to a place of acceptance.

Miracles have a habit of arriving when least expected. The morning after I was admitted, the doctor marched into my room and said, "We think we've identified a donor." I was scared, happy and, most of all relieved, until the magnitude of it all began to sink in. My twisted gratitude instantly shifted from agitated waiting and wondering to a whirlwind of preparation. Craig and I were briefed by several hospital staffers and visited by a social worker; a woman who explained the procurement process and the critical role the agency plays for both the organ recipient and the donor's family. Confidentiality demanded I be given only limited information about my donor— age, gender, and geographical region. The donor family is given the same limited information—just enough to assure the organ(s) went to good use. It is an immensely difficult time, especially for the donor's family. So, by keeping personal data confidential, no one on either side can make or receive unwelcome contact. Often times, because the process is so intensely emotional, both parties are eager to move on. For me, the mystery had just begun.

From the hospital's perspective, when a heart becomes available, it's a big deal for everyone—patients, doctors, nurses, and staff. A joyful buzz resonates throughout the CCU. A life can be saved. Then follows a chilling silence, everyone listening to the whirring blades of a helicopter taking off for a nearby hospital to recover the donor heart. Craig and I felt caught in-between, more anxious than excited, but distracted by the chore of filling out a flurry of consent forms for surgery, directives, consultations, blood work, etc. The bits of information we'd been provided about my donor played over and over in my mind. She was a forty-year-old mother, and had died from head injuries sustained in a horseback riding accident. She was my size, petite, and had been six years older than me. All I wanted to focus on was that she had been *active* and *healthy.* I didn't want to know more about her, didn't want to personalize the heart that might be beating inside me. I feared any emotional attachment, or guilt associated with the fact that she died and I was saved. My concern was that such agonizing could compromise my physical strength during the operation. I shifted my focus away from any thoughts of the pending surgery and the larger issues attached to it. I did what comes naturally to me whenever I'm facing the unknown, a trait I've inherited from my father: I thought about my next meal. In the back of my mind, I must have known an NPO sign (abbreviated Latin for "nothing by mouth") would soon be dangling above my bed, indicating no food or drink. Still, I kept my worried mind occupied with rich, colorful fantasies of my "final" meal.

TJ arrived, providing a great distraction not only for me, but also for Craig and my parents. Expertly skilled as a nurse at comforting families, she proved invaluable at maintaining a sense of calm and creating a positive aura. She told them, "I have said this to many people, and I will forever say it: Kelly overcomes her physical pain with more grace and less visible effort than anyone I've ever seen. Her commitment to physical endeavors has always been beyond anyone I've met—man or woman. Any physical challenge she is passionate about, she overcomes. I'll never forget seeing the bruises on her hips from carrying her skis on our first backpack trip. She acted as if the bruises were no big deal, but they were—three inches round on each hip— and she had to put the pack right on top of them to hike back!" She convinced them I would fight and win.

Later that afternoon, we were told the surgery was scheduled for 6:00 P.M. But as the hour grew near, we experienced the first of several delays. We were on hold until the harvest team recovered the donor's heart from the place where she'd passed. The delay was requested on behalf of the donor's family and, obviously, with all due respect, we were happy to honor that. I tried to doze off, knowing I wouldn't be taken down to the Operating

Room and prepped until the organ arrived. I tried to focus on anything but the looming surgery and my roaring hunger pangs. In the meantime, I was given a mild sedative to keep me calm.

I was told to stay on alert standby, knowing they could come at any time to take me to the OR. I envisioned the helicopter blades cutting a cyclonic path through the twilight air, dramatically heralding the arrival of the precious cargo on board.

Finally at midnight, I was called to action. On the way to the OR, it was explained to me that I would not be given anesthesia or cut open until the heart was on the premises, and only after my surgeon approved it for transplant. In other words, I might find myself back in my room, the surgery scrubbed. I was calm, refusing to dwell on what might happen either way. My parents and TJ wished me well from the elevator, and Craig came along as far he could until he reached the restricted area. He kissed me and whispered a promise to see me later, purposely avoiding the word "good-bye."

The room was so cold it felt like a refrigerator. I lay in the bed, reminding myself *the heart still needs the surgeon's blessing*. I waited for what seemed like mere moments, feeling remarkably relaxed. For the first time in a long time, I didn't have to devote each waking second to outmaneuvering death. At this point, my life was out of my hands. Finally, I heard the words "it's good, let's go." Seconds later, I was fast asleep. Knowing they'd be waiting a long time for me to emerge from the OR, my dad made his usual suggestion to Craig, inviting him out for a bite to eat. With a nervous laugh, he quipped, "While Kelly may be NPO, I'm certainly not."

Mom and TJ opted to stay in the waiting room while Craig chaperoned Dad to a nearby all-night diner, the

Beverly Hills Café. The circumstances would strain most appetites, but never my dad's. While Craig, understandably terrified, hardly touched his hamburger, dad demonstrated his nervousness the opposite way, by cleaning his plate. Revealing his sweetly sentimental side, dad held on to the receipt from their meal, treasuring the time stamp that marked one of the most important periods of his life. He subsequently had this receipt framed, and it now hangs prominently in the stairwell of their home.

At 3:00 A.M, Craig, my parents, and TJ were provided their first update. The heart was transplanted. At 4:30 A.M., they were told I'd been taken off the heart/lung machine and my new heart was beating on it's own. At 5:30 A.M., I was wheeled into the ICU. At 6:00 A.M., I groggily awoke to the vision of Craig and dad (only two visitors were allowed at one time) hovering anxiously over me. Because I was so highly immunocompromised, they were suited up in gloves, gowns, and masks. They looked like curious little kids waiting for me to stir. I managed a trembling "thumbs up." I was OK.

CHAPTER 6

Wireless

IT would have been naïve to expect an event-free recovery, especially after transplant surgery. I was installed in the ICU, where one nurse's sole responsibility was to watch over me. Intravenous medications and antibiotics supported my new heart. To minimize potential risk to my weakened immune system, few visitors were allowed in, so Craig, TJ, and my parents each took turns. Most of the time, I dozed between the many tests that closely monitored my progress.

A waist-high solid wall, topped with clear glass that extended all the way to the ceiling, bordered my high-tech room. The see-through design allowed the nurses to quickly spot a patient in need and respond instantly. Fortunately, I was flat on my back, so unable to observe the condition of some of the others around me. Craig, on the other hand, was in direct view of some fairly horrific scenes. He told me later, in perhaps too vivid detail, about the man waiting for a heart in the space adjacent to mine. He was in such bad shape they kept his chest cavity surgically propped open, with just a few wet towels covering his flesh and organs, because his heart required frequent hands-on assistance. Like trying to stare away from a horrible car accident, Craig would find his eyes inadvertently wandering toward the scene of the wreck, each time quickly snapping back to take comfort in seeing me in a comparably less gruesome state. As dire as my neighbor's situation appeared, the fact remained that he, too, was a lucky one: he was still alive. A freshly empty bed in the ICU was such a discomforting sight. It was an odd environment to recover in, with death and new life crowding the same space.

Throughout my first day, I remained in a drugged delirium and didn't feel much at all. While I was sleeping, Craig left the room to rest in the nearby lounge. I woke up, alone and panicked. I felt trapped by all the attached paraphernalia and couldn't find the energy to move. Terrified, I asked for Craig to be paged. Surrounded by beeping high-tech devices, I felt transported to a sci-fi movie. More freakish than that—I felt my heart! The powerful surge against my jagged chest incision, which seemed held together by a too-thin bandage, was alarmingly strong, and with each powerful beat, I visualized it jumping right out. The beat was so thundering, all I could focus on was the pounding in my ears. It was like a booming car stereo in my chest, going thump, thump, thump. I was alarmed enough to call in the doctor, insisting that, "something is wrong!" It didn't feel right. Should I be *feeling* my heart? Maybe, just maybe, they'd screwed up. I even wondered if they'd put it in upside down! Then, as if my nerves weren't raw enough, I began to have rapid heartbeats. I thought, "Oh my God, after everything I've been through, they've given me back my old heart!" I figured, with all the pandemonium associated with such a complicated surgery, that it wasn't too farfetched to wonder if they'd taken my old heart out, placed it on the same table next to the new heart, and then inadvertently put it back in. I became obsessed with this bizarre theory. Because Craig was nearly comatose with exhaustion, he didn't hear the nurses' pages. As he peacefully slept, I became more and more freaked out. When he finally did wake up, he looked down at his pager and saw I'd tried to reach him five times. He rushed into the ICU, where I frantically told him, "I got a bum heart." Soon after, the doctor stopped by to quell my fears, reassuring us that the surgery was successful and my heart was just going through a period of adjustment.

Keeping his promise to never leave my side, Craig would hide from the ICU nurses as visitors' hours ended, spending the next few nights *under* my bed. Frequently, he would reach up his hand and grasp mine, gently reminding me that he was there for me.

As my new heart and I adjusted to one another, there were fresh issues to deal with, including a powerful, new pump pounding in my chest, toxic doses of entirely new drug cocktails, the insertion of painful knifelike tubes to equalize pressure resulting from air pockets in my chest cavity, and wild blood pressure swings, from high to low, causing piercing migraines. All such side effects were uncomfortable, but bearable. What mattered most was the knowledge that I'd made it though the hard part.

With time, I grew convinced my heart was healthy and, given the chance, would adapt to its new space. Then, just as it seemed everything was ticking along as it should, the first of many biopsies revealed my body was rejecting my new heart. I immediately became despondent. My body was rebelling—*now* it was putting up a fight. I was sick of this game. An insidious virus had gotten me into this mess in the first place. Where in the hell was my immune system then? Having been so good to my body, I could only ask myself, "What kind of payback is this?"

We had been warned about rejection, told it wasn't uncommon for transplant patients to experience at least one episode. As emotionally unsettling as the news was, the longer I pondered it the more I began to accept it. Intellectually, I could understand my body's reaction, appreciating that it had been totally violated and was, of course, going to fight back. After all, the new organ was foreign to my body, and like an unwelcome sliver, my body's instinctive response was to try to get rid of it. Attempting to allay my fear, my new cardiologist, Dr. Jon Kobashigawa, assured me they had all kinds of ammunition, meaning drugs, to combat the T-cells that were attacking my new heart. The first line of defense involved high doses of intravenous steroids, toxic miracle drugs whose side effects included a puffy "moon" face. This little hiccup meant I would be skipping another holiday, spending Thanksgiving in the hospital. But I wasn't alone; Craig and my family were also missing out. It was tough to imagine that, on the one day of the year my mother allowed it, my dad would have to forego his belly-busting Thanksgiving pig-out. So, making the best of the situation, we decided to have our own little celebration. Craig made his way down to the ground floor cafeteria to load up plates of fresh-carved turkey breast with all the trimmings, but returned sooner than expected with bad news: they were all out of it. By this point, I was having a hard time feeling thankful for anything at all.

I was finally released to go home on Friday, December 1, 1995. Freedom at last! As a homecoming gift, Craig worked with Jim, a family friend who is a jeweler to create a heart-shaped pendant, crafted of silver, gold and three small rubies. Depicted in silver and gold was my new heart rising out of my tired, old broken heart. The rubies represented the trio of Craig, Dr. Cannom, and me. It was a beautiful reminder of my, and our, new beginning.

Although it was a typical Southern California winter, with sunny skies and pleasant temperatures in the high 50s, I seemed to be cold all the time. Having been reduced to a meager eighty-nine pounds of a heart, skin, and bones didn't help. Craig took me to one of our favorite sporting goods stores, REI, to buy some expedition-weight long johns, but I had a hard time opening the package, afraid I may never need them. I felt I should wait until my next biopsy, just to make sure.

Returning to UCLA for my first outpatient biopsy turned out to be an experience straight out of *One Flew Over the Cuckoo's Nest*. I was required to go to the transplant clinic every two weeks, in a facility near the hospital that serves mainly new heart recipients, all flying high on a combination of doctor-prescribed Prednisone and a fierce, self-prescribed determination to live. The biopsy area has two procedure rooms. Between them, folding chairs are set up for waiting patients casually attired in sweats or a hospital gown, and wearing a disposable paper mask to help ward off germs. I was never eager to wait, not due to a lack of patience, but because of the nagging complaining and endless comparison of symptoms, associated medical issues, medications, etc. Hardest to take was the age-related bragging. Several of the "golden-age" recipients felt the need to issue constant reminders of their donor's youthfulness, somehow believing that becoming the owner of a seventeen-year-old's heart could make them a teenager all over again. In my case, my donor was six years my senior. There I was, usually the youngest recipient in the room, with one of the oldest hearts. I knew *in my heart* that I was still young while they were still old. Deep down we were all enormously grateful to be among the lucky ones who'd received a transplant.

Since my stomach had to be empty for the biopsy and blood draw, I always tried to be first in line so I could then go eat. Traffic is always an issue in Southern California. To be on the safe side, we'd leave home at 5:30 A.M., ahead of most commuters. Because we were in so early, we were able to leave by 2:00 P.M., again missing the heaviest traffic, leaving just enough time for a tranquil stroll around Balboa Island before a quiet dinner at home.

After that first biopsy, Craig and I wandered down to the beach for a leisurely walk, and then ran some errands. We were only gone a few hours, but arrived home to three messages on the answering machine. Sure enough, all three were from the hospital. The first said, "Kelly, this is UCLA, please call." The second was from the transplant coordinator, her voice building with tension as she insisted, "Kelly, you need to call right away." The third was alarming. Her voice was abrupt as she demanded, "Kelly, we have your results. You need to check into emergency and be admitted."

Craig hurriedly packed up the car and we raced to UCLA, checking in for what would be *another* fourteen days of high-dose IV steroids. Instead of being happy about my short flight to freedom, I was disillusioned it was all coming to an end. Also, I was about to endure a drug treatment that would further suppress my immune system. My vulnerability to disease would be as severe as that of an AIDS patient. The thought of knocking out my protection in a germ and virus-infested hospital environment was daunting. I would be left completely naked, in direct proximity to the most virulent of diseases. Understandably, I was freaked out.

Then came more bad news. The hospital census was full—I would need to share a room. Now I was worried about germs my roommate or her visitors might be carrying. To make matters worse, my roommate scored a giant zero on the coolness scale. She moaned and groaned when she was alone and, if she needed to talk, would pick up the phone, regardless of the time. If she was suffering, so was everyone else. It was impossible not to hear her as, late into the night, she exercised her dubious parenting skills via telephone. I initially thought she was being unruly because of the drugs, but quickly came to see her true nature: über-bitch in attack mode. It was day two, 3:00 A.M., and she screamed into the phone, "When I get out of here, I am going to knock you to hell and back." Her screeching diatribe went on and on. I wasn't in the mood and had no patience for this. Craig had even less.

Craig's hygiene was wearing as thin as his patience. He had a ragged t-shirt he'd purchased years earlier in Hawaii that said "West Wind, Dive Kauai " across the chest. He washed it as rarely as he changed it, insisting it was his "lucky" shirt. From time to time, both my mother and TJ commented on the shirt's increasingly foul smell of aging perspiration. Mom pushed the point, remarking, "After all we have been through, how can you possibly think that shirt brings *luck*," but Craig wasn't about to part with his odorous security blanket.

One day, while taking a short walk near UCLA, Craig noticed a few men in business suits, apparently returning to their offices from lunch at one of the many restaurants near the campus. As they drew closer, he recognized one of them as a college friend, now an attorney, and yelled out to him, "Pat, hi." Pat looked at him as though he was some homeless dude. Finally he put Craig's voice and our situation together and realized who the bedraggled stranger was. He was utterly shocked. Craig looked thin, sloppy, pale, unshaven, and frankly, beaten up.

It had become visibly evident, Craig was suffering as severely as I was.

Knowing we were going to be in the hospital for some time, Craig inquired about a private room. By this point, our medical bills were exorbitant, but debt was a low priority, as it could be paid off in the future. His immediate and only concern was my comfort and safety. However, a private room was not easy to come by, as they were typically used only if the census was full or for VIPs such as government officials or Hollywood personalities. UCLA's fourth floor, where I was required to stay because of the monitoring equipment, had only two, and both were occupied. Spending another two or more weeks in the hospital was hard enough to deal with. Sharing all that time with my witch of a roommate was beyond comprehension. Luckily, Craig overheard that one of the private rooms was coming available, and made it his mission to secure it for me. Learning that another patient was vying for the same room, Craig sprang into action. While the one patient was making their bid through the floor nurse, Craig dashed directly to the billing department and threw down his credit card to lock up the deal. The room paid for, it couldn't be assigned to anyone else.

Ah, privacy and a good night sleep, at last! Though the new room was as stark and plain as the one I'd just vacated, I felt like I'd been transferred from a mountain-side emergency clinic to a five-star resort. It was spacious, blessedly quiet, and provided much greater control over germs that might enter. Things were looking up for Craig, too. He could comfortably sleep near me in a reclining gurney he'd commandeered from an area storage room. Best of all, he was released from food duty. As it turned out, the hospital was comparable to a jumbo jet. Staying in a private room was like sitting in first class, complete with gourmet meals. I could have whatever I wanted to eat, whenever I was hungry. To top it off, the meals were prepared in a completely different kitchen, by a wonderfully creative chef who was happy to customize each meal to my specific tastes. There was still no candlelight, but now my meal arrived under a silver dome, and my tray was adorned with a linen tablecloth, a matching napkin and sterling silver utensils. Wow, I felt like I had died and gone to, well, hospital heaven.

Although catering to my dietary needs had been crossed off Craig's "to-do" list, each night he took a fifteen-minute stroll to a nearby campus store and bought us both a frozen treat. One evening, while walking around Westwood Village, he came across an intriguing gift shop. Browsing around, he caught sight of cute little glow-in-the-dark angels, promoted as stickers for kids. He initially thought of our godchild, Casey, knowing she would love them. Then he thought of me. What a perfect gift to help keep me relaxed. He was so thrilled with his purchase that, upon his return, he immediately jumped up onto the bed and started adhering the angels to the ceiling. We waited excitedly for it to turn dark outside so we could extinguish the lights and share the sweet sensation of angels watching over me.

On December 23, with a clear biopsy, I was released to go home for Christmas with strict instructions not to return for seven days. Overjoyed to be released before the holiday, we made a beeline to the exit. Naturally, my parents stayed to add to our holiday cheer. On Christmas Eve day, Craig and my dad ventured to a tree lot, only to find it vacant. The only thing left was a large dumpster filled with discarded trees that hadn't found a home. Knowing how important it was for me, and for all of us, to have a tree—*any* tree—Craig climbed inside the dumpster while

dad, riddled with his Catholic guilt that they were breaking the law, waited in the car. Craig rifled through the discarded branches and spiky pine needles, finally uncovering
something that vaguely resembled a Christmas tree. A
genuine "Charlie Brown" special, it wasn't going to support many ornaments, but its fragrance would not only
enhance our festive mood but also remind us that every
living thing, no matter how damaged, was worth saving.
We erected the tree in our living room and decorated it
with a single strand of flickering mini-lights. It was perfect. When I awoke the next morning, I looked under the
tree and saw that it was full of gifts Craig had purchased
and wrapped for everyone. Since he had been by my side
in the hospital nearly every waking moment, I couldn't
imagine how he found time to purchase the presents,
much less wrap them. He had even bought presents for
himself, knowing I was in no position to get him anything. I adored how goofy he acted, gleefully tearing the
wrapping off his gifts and yelling with surprised excitement at what he found inside each package. Among the
gifts was an item all four of us shared—sweatshirts from
the campus gift store, emblazoned with "UCLA Medical
Center." Our festive morning continued in a light vein,
until Craig handed me a special gift he'd been saving for
last. It was a charm bracelet, naked of charms. I instantly
knew what I would fill it with—mountains! It would be
a splendid array of mountain charms, each representing a
new peak I would conquer with my new heart.

My seven hospital-free days came to an end when I
returned for my next required biopsy. To the frustration
of even my doctors, my body seemed to have defied the
toughest defenses as it was discovered I was back in rejection. I was so over it! The arsenal of options nearly
depleted, I was forced to explore a new drug, one that

was not yet given a brand name, called FK506, along with a new, unconventional treatment called photophresis, rather like a cross between dialysis and chemotherapy. It was done twice a week over a period of six months, on an outpatient basis. The treatments took place in a small hospital room with three other beds, typically filled with cancer patients receiving chemotherapy. Each session began with a morning dose of a radioactive drug, followed by six hours hooked up to a special blood-processing machine. A pint of blood was taken from me, put through a centrifuge, spun to separate the red from the white cells, leaving only the white cells exposed to UV light, thereby sterilizing them. Once sterile, the blood had nothing to fight back with, and through a catheter the "peaceful" cold blood was put back into my veins. While it wasn't a completely experimental procedure, I was only the second heart transplant recipient at UCLA to go through it. After an intense battle with the insurance company, they finally agreed to recognize this as a "medically necessary" treatment and cover the high cost. Thank goodness, because this new drug and cutting-edge treatment was the silver bullet—the turning point that finally got me out of the woods. Just a few months into treatment, I was no longer in rejection.

During one of my photophresis visits, Craig went up to the cardiac floor to gather a supply of protection masks for me, and ran into Stephanie, one of our former nurses. As soon as she saw him, she began laughing, saying, "Have I got a story for you!" She went on to tell Craig that after I was discharged in December, they wheeled a man straight from surgery into the private room we had previously occupied. As the anesthesia began to wear off, he started yelling to the nurse that he was sure he was dying because he was seeing angels. When the nurse came running in and flipped on the lights, he said the angels were gone. Confused, the nurse proceeded to turn out the lights as she exited the room. Moments later, the patient began screaming anew. The nurse ran in the room again and tried to calm him, explaining that he was still coming off his medication and was not dying. He was desperate and started rambling. He told her that every time she left the room, the angels appeared to collect him. Finally, after much investigation, the nurse looked up at the ceiling and discovered our host of paste-on, glow-in-the-dark seraphim.

After several months, my biopsies continued to appear free of rejection. We were back home now, searching for normalcy. It wasn't so easy. We were both so use to being on constant alert, either putting out an emergency medical fire or waiting for the next one to flare up. I was so focused on my physical recovery, pushing any emotional or spiritual concerns to the deepest recesses of my mind, that I was ill prepared for what happened next. I convinced myself I was done with being in a perpetual funk. Done, done, done. Unfortunately, because so many aspects of my life had so radically changed, I couldn't simply "move on."

I have heard of patients experiencing the transplant process in the same way one experiences grief, following the similar stages. Looking back, there was as much light as shadow. Initially, I had *fought* having a heart transplant, resisting the idea of major surgery because I retained hope my birth heart could, and would, make a comeback. When I went into congestive heart failure, I made the personal decision to fight *for* a new heart, finally *accepting* that I needed it to survive. Once I received the new heart, I was *guarded* about it: it seemed foreign, somehow not right. Then, just as my heart and I were getting to know one another, my new heart went into severe rejection. There was no motivation for me to make emotional room for an organ that my body was rebelling against, a heart I might easily lose. Even after the rejection cleared, and the new heart started working for me, I treated it as *borrowed*, not yet my own. I've since been told of women who have a similar reaction while pregnant, experiencing that same sense of tentativeness, perhaps afraid to get too close to the child they're carrying in case of a miscarriage. There was a long period of adjustment. I told myself I wasn't going to accept this heart until I knew for sure it was going to work for, and with, me. My body and my donor heart needed to cooperate as partners.

I felt it was extremely important to send a thank you note to the donor's family. Time and again, I sat down and tried to shape the right words, but could never quite manage to convey how I really felt. I set a goal, with the letter finally going out on Valentine's Day.

To my surprise, shortly after I mailed the note, I got a response. It turned out the donor's sister had sent a Christmas card to us months earlier, but the card had been held by the organ procurement agency, who forwarded it to me only after I showed interest in making a connection. As an aside, I respect an organization that recognizes the sensitivity of the situation, and takes the initiative to look after the emotional well-being of parties on both sides. While many recipients want to establish a friendship, or even build a family-type relationship, with their donor's family, I was hoping our exchange of letters would provide a sense of closure for all concerned.

Craig was typically creative in helping accelerate my acceptance of my new heart. He understood my inherent desire to be, and appear, a fit, healthy person, and worked with me to set goals to reward my mind and body through physical accomplishments. He replaced his recurring "How do you feel?" with "What's the best part of your day, so far?"

At the time, during the early stages of post transplantation, the protocol was to wear a disposable paper mask in public areas, establishing a protective barrier between me and spores, dust, bacteria, colds and flu. The philosophy has since changed, the level of protection the masks provide now debatable. Still, because it was recommended, I complied. As a result, there was no way to go out during this period without calling attention to myself. At times, it was quite embarrassing. I just wanted to blend in with the rest of humanity.

I find it intriguing that most people have an angelic image of those who have been through a medical crisis. I always find it humorous, especially when I'm having a bad day, to hear, "You must be so appreciative of every minute of every day." Strangers expect me to be unrealistically "centered." I feel like they're counting on me to turn into a walking, talking greeting card, regardless of what's going on in my life.

Undergoing a successful transplant is, without doubt, a life-affirming experience. Yet, while I can be appreciative, I can also be nasty. I have way too much that I want to accomplish and, if you're in my way, you'd better watch out! It's not a side of me I'm particularly proud of; but my "ugly face" will show if I'm feeling overly anxious or hurried. I can overreact to the same things that drive us all a little crazy, like a person holding up a long line by paying for a single bagel with a credit card, or rudely oblivious cell phone users, and I have a special intolerance for time-consuming voicemail prompts that lead you through a maze of "press 1 for . . . press 2 for . . ." I remember my nerves being rubbed raw during an insurance claim call. After listening to an annoying prerecorded voice telling me where to find the "pound" button on my receiver, I yelled a nasty swear word, a word not normally in my vocabulary. The automated system responded in its creepy, computer-generated monotone, "I am sorry, I don't understand that response. Just one moment please, I will get an operator." And with that, my new access code, I was able to talk to a real, live person!

During this time, I became overprotective of my physical self, fearful of being too active. I imagined my heart to be incredibly delicate, as if attached by the slightest of threads, and was afraid to exert myself in any way. As I began to exercise a bit more and return to normal daily activities, I discovered there was a significant delay between any activity I engaged in and my heart rate's increase. Because I immediately went into rejection after the transplant, it became the urgent focus. As such, I was never told that my heart was now "denervated." During the surgery, the nerves are severed and, because there is no way to reattach them, there's no longer a connection to the brain. Although it would present some cardiac limitations, in time my body would adapt. The news, however, that I was now "wired differently" came as quite a shock!

Here's a simple, but vivid, example of how my new heart functions. As I ascend a standard staircase, my heart rate remains at a resting rate, typically taking anywhere from two to ten minutes before the requisite added beats kick in. Without the additional oxygen fueling my deprived muscles, I quickly become completely out of breath, as winded as a marathon runner who has hit the wall. The reverse is also true. Just as my heart does not sense to speed up when exertion is necessary, it also experiences a delay when I stop or slow down. As a result, my blood pressure increases, heading straight for my brain and often causing a migraine-strength headache. It all seems so backwards, but drives home to me how powerful the physiological effects of a straightforward stair climb could be.

This heart-brain connection fascinates me. The human body is, of course, a marvel of engineering. The nervous system is beautifully wired, with a direct connection from brain to heart. For a heart transplant recipient, this unique link—different from the brain's connection to any other organ—doesn't exist. As a result, my heart is not automatically piloted by my nervous system. It is like a car engine without a starter.

Fortunately, the body has it's own, built-in backup— the adrenaline system. That's how my engine now gets started. As I get active, my muscles become deprived of the oxygen they need, triggering the "fight or flight" response. This causes a release of adrenaline, thereby inducing an increase in heart rate to accommodate for my level of exertion. It's very efficient, but not as quick to respond, thus the two- to ten-minute delay. It would take significant time to get used to, but I was determined to do so. I wanted to get to know my heart. Coming face to face with death had given me a new fierceness. I told Craig, "I'm no longer afraid of dying; I'm afraid of *not living*."

Literally step-by-step, I gradually increased my physical activity, eager to exchange stifling hospital rooms for sunlit mountain trails. To keep me motivated, Craig constantly reinforced the idea that, having survived what we'd been through, we could conquer anything. He supported my fervent desire to get back to the mountains, knowing that my passion needed to outpace my fear. I soon realized the mountains would become my very best medicine. Through training, I was able to minimize any nagging "what ifs." It was humbling and frustrating at first, walking our cul-de-sac and being overtaken by an eighty-year old, but I stuck with it. With time and patience, I increased my frequency, distance and level of difficulty, all in an effort to build endurance.

Within six months, I was able to regain a lot of my physical energy. On May 1, 1996, Craig and I made a trip to Lake Tahoe. It was an emotional return. Because of the altitude, it was the first time I'd been able to visit my family's home since my initial diagnosis, four years earlier. The decreased oxygen levels in higher elevations can cause the heart to work harder, which would have put added stress on my already compromised organ. Around every corner was a reminder that this is where Craig and I had spent much of our carefree, courtship years. While we were there, we took advantage of the opportunity to venture back to Echo Lake, the very same area where we made our first backpack trip together. This time, the goal was simple, to take the shuttle boat across the lake and see how my new ticker would respond to the 7,000-foot elevation. The day was much shorter than our first visit, back in 1982, but was filled with even more nervous excitement, ignited by our shared belief that, for the second time, it marked the beginning of a bright future.

CHAPTER 7

Bubbles over Half Dome

IKE life, mountains can be seen as a series of splendid obstacles. To me, a mountain is the ultimate challenge, with body, spirit, and mind all having to work together. Being sick is, too. Both involve bravely facing the unknown, and to conquer either requires well-defined goals, discipline, and compliance. Of the two, of course, I'd rather the mountain be my physical challenge than physical challenges be my mountain.

Mountains began to consume my thoughts. Secretly, I wanted to do something significant to help change the image that friends and family had developed of me and also the image I'd formed of myself. By way of example, form a mental image of Henry Winkler. What do you think of? A guy named Fonzie in a black leather jacket, motorcycling his way through an episode of *Happy Days*, right? Well, just as that one character has come to define, and confine, the actor, I had been cast in the role of patient. In spite of being very good in that role, I despised the association and desperately wanted to change my image. I wanted bruises to be earned from sports-related activities, not from needle pricks and aspirin-thinned blood. At this stage, my self-image was as important, if not more, to my well-being than anything else. If, I figured, I could rebuild my strength and regain at least some of my former athleticism; an improved image would naturally follow.

I set a goal—to hike the 4,100-foot ascent of Half Dome in Yosemite. I was drawn to this destination by its beauty, a beauty derived not from its perfection but from its imperfection. Half Dome's shape is unforgettably distinctive because it's broken. If it were whole, it would lose its uniqueness. The spirit-building message wasn't lost on me. Just because I wasn't perfect, didn't mean I couldn't stand as tall and mighty as anyone else.

At the beginning of August 1996, Craig and I went on our first true backpack trip to prepare for Half Dome. We decided to go to the eastern side of the Sierras to hike in the scenic area of Agnew Meadows. Cresting the 9,000-foot pass, I felt exhilarated; as if I had earned back the life that I had loved and lost. It was invigorating to have the strength to don a backpack, though a much lighter model than the hip-bruising ones of my past, and to resubmerge myself in familiar trails.

The new level of stamina I achieved on the Agnew Meadows hike gave Craig and me the confidence that our planned Half Dome trip was not too farfetched. Without revealing our true agenda, we decided to coordinate the event around a group annual trip. Marking our fourteenth year together, with a few "medical" misses in-between, it would be an event worthy of a group reunion. We chose the Redwoods in Yosemite National Park as our home base. In the past, our group annuals were built around grueling, marathon marches carrying heavy backpacks across miles and miles of difficult mountain terrain. But times had changed. I was still somewhat frail, after four years of illness and just ten months after my transplant. Our friends had their own demands—high-maintenance babies and toddlers who couldn't be toted but weren't yet capable of hiking on their own—hence the replacement of backpacks and tents for SUVs and cabins.

Though our mates needed to be a little more cabin-bound, now that there were munchkins in the picture, it wasn't going to inhibit our goal. While I was excited to resume sharing time with people I cherished, I knew everyone would be arranging babysitting schedules and catching up with much-needed sleep.

On the second day, we invited a few pals to join us on a short trek. For Craig and me, it was to be a "warm up" hike. We'd heard there were impressive waterfalls near our cabin, and easily rallied five companions to join us. We hiked single file up a narrow, dusty, tree-lined trail in 80-degree heat, pointed toward falls that were, we'd been told, "just up a little ways." We could hear the rushing water, but couldn't see it. Everything made sense four miles later, when we finally arrived and felt the mist from the water's spray. The falls alone were worth the hike, but because we could now see the source of the down rush, we decided to continue on to the top. A short distance further, we came upon a stream that fed and filled granite pockets, creating icy cold plunge pools. As a reward for their efforts, the guys stripped down to their skivvies and jumped into the refreshing water. I was a bit more hesitant, not just due to my aversion to swimming, but out of fear of not knowing what kind of contaminants the raw water might harbor, concerned about problems they could potentially cause with my suppressed immune system. The short rest helped us all gain a second wind, even though we had very little to drink. Because our original intent was to hike only a short distance, as opposed to the eight-mile roundtrip we ultimately endured, no one thought to bring much water. After the hike, everyone headed back to the cabins to "hydrate," replacing lost fluids with a few cold beers. Craig and I decided to pass on the beer fest, preserving our energy and focusing on our discreet goal of hiking Half Dome the following day.

We left very early in the morning, hoping to make it back in time for dinner. Craig kept reminding me of our agreement: if at any time I felt weak or tired, we'd turn around. After all, this hike was intended strictly for fun, just to see how far we could get. Before making the trip, Craig sent a letter to Nike and REI asking for a few pieces of equipment in support of my climb. Both recognized the immensity of the challenge and graciously offered to send some complimentary items. It wasn't the material value of what they provided so much as what their support represented. As Craig said, "Nike only sponsors athletes, so clearly you are no longer sick." He innately knew it was precisely the sort of psychological image boost I needed.

During our approach to the trailhead, which began from the Happy Isles area in the valley, we saw first hand the devastation from the recent rock fall, just two months earlier. Reminiscent of Mount St. Helen's, the massive force of the impact had toppled more than three hundred trees across ten acres, killing one person. The beginning of the trail was like being in a black and white movie, as all color was buried beneath a layer of grey ash from the exploding rocks. It was a startling reminder of life's eternal cycle, continuously building up and tearing down.

The trail began with a mild incline, which we eagerly took at a brisk pace. I was winded at first, but as soon as my heart caught up with me, I felt energized. I tried to go at the same clip as the surrounding hikers, but found it difficult to keep up as we bordered the Mist Trail along the steep bank of Vernal and Nevada Falls. The canyon, full of sharp vertical inclines and deep stone stairs, allowed in very little sunlight, which kept temperatures cool and the rocks slippery. Nearing the top of the falls, where the terrain leveled off, we came across a couple in their late sixties. We waved and said "hello," admiring that they'd made it so far up. The woman was limping along slowly enough for us to pass her. I whispered to Craig, "Wow, just like old times—passing someone twice my age!" She was moaning and groaning. As they continued along, her husband proudly explained, "My wife is struggling a bit—she recently had a hip replacement." Craig couldn't resist replying, "That's terrific you are both out here. I can relate, as my wife just had a *heart* replacement." They stared coldly at Craig. It wasn't immediately clear if they believed him or thought he was making light of her pain with such a tasteless joke. Slowly, the realization dawned that he was telling the truth. Craig and I smiled as they immediately picked up their pace. That brief, bizarre conversation made me all the more determined to make it all the way to the top.

Over lunch, we relaxed and caught our breath. It was then we discovered my backpack's hydration system, filled with water, had sprung a leak, draining all its precious fluid. Though the temperature was approaching 90 degrees, we decided to continue our quest to conquer the summit. We were only one mile from the top, and figured we could share Craig's remaining water; not realizing it was four miles to the nearest stream.

Though the climb's final half-mile isn't technically difficult, the granite dome, angled at 45 degrees, can be extremely intimidating, especially for those afraid of heights. The last 500 feet to the summit looks like the "stairway to heaven." Two steel cables, approximately 4 feet tall, are strung along intermittent poles to create a makeshift handrail, connected to stairs made of thin wooden planks. Sprawled about are old, weathered work gloves, available to trekkers' to help protect their hands from the "death grip" commonly used during descent. Craig, observing the daunting task ahead, gently asked, "Are you sure you want to continue?" Determined to reap the reward for all my effort, I resolutely replied, "Absolutely, we have to go on." Step for step, Craig stayed directly behind me, providing a welcome sense of security. When I finally reached the top, I was overcome with joy. Ten months after my transplant, I had summated Half Dome! My new heart had not let me down.

Apparently, thanks to Craig's boasting, word had already reached the summit that a heart transplant recipient was on her way. Four middle-aged women gleefully identified me as "the one." They dashed toward us, congratulating me on my accomplishment. Anne, Connie, Donie, and Joanne had been friends since their college days, and shared their own annual adventure, similar to what we do with our pals. They shared with us their tradition of celebrating momentous events by blowing bubbles and making wishes. "Would you join us in making a wish?" Jo asked as she presented me with a plastic bubble wand. As I made my wish our bubbles joined together and floated over the granite edge and off into the clear blue sky. I felt as weightless and free as those soapy spheres. A magical moment with strangers, with the self-dubbed "bubble ladies," highlighted how impactful this trek was.

Craig and I made our way over to the massive cliff edge. Pausing to peer into the valley below, we stood in silence, in awe of how far we had come. As if the moment itself was not enough, Craig surprised me with a gold charm in the shape of Half Dome. He said, "This is the first mountain to add to the bracelet I gave you for

Christmas." As I held the handcrafted ornament in my hand, I was amazed at its likeness. It was smooth on the back, resembling the perfectly bell-shaped dome; the front being chiseled, replicating its famous broken granite edifice. As I doted on it's form, Craig explained how he'd had it made. He'd set out on his quest months earlier. He began by calling the souvenir shop in Yosemite Village, but they had nothing resembling a charm of Half Dome. The only thing they had was a replica of the mountain inside a clear plastic snow dome. He decided it was his best bet, and shipped the dome to our jeweler friend Jim. He asked him to break open the plastic bubble and use the mountain inside as a three-dimensional model, and replicate it in the form of a miniature gold charm. Needless to say, such effort and resourcefulness only added to its priceless appeal. Returning the precious memento to his pocket, Craig took a moment to express how proud he was of me, saying "When you were really sick and I had to carry you up the stairs at night, I always looked at the famous Ansel Adams photo of Half Dome hung on the stairway wall and wondered if we'd ever make another climb." His tender words brought me to tears. We had done it; we were here at the top of the mountain—a long way from those nights of desperate uncertainty.

It was closing in on 2:00 P.M. and we knew we had to hustle down. This would be the dicey part—the severe drop-off of the cable section. It wasn't the exposure that became intimidating, but the traffic congestion—navigating our way between the people on their way up and dealing with one woman in particular. Utterly freaked out, she stood dead still with her grip frozen on the cables, blocking everyone moving up or down.

After disentangling ourselves from the human traffic jam at the cables, we made our way to the better-defined trail. Little did we know that our charmed celebration was about to prove short lived. I began to feel fatigued. It started with stomach cramps, causing me to dash into the bushes and relieve myself, only to discover I was at the early stages of dehydration. To make matters worse, Craig's fluid supply was now nearly depleted and we were still miles from the closest stream. It was becoming clear to us that our unexpectedly long trek the previous day had exhausted my energy reserve. I tried to maintain my composure and keep a decent pace, focusing on my immediate goal to get to the river. It seemed like forever before we finally heard the sound of running water. Craig rushed ahead to purify and refill our hydration packs, while I continued down the path. Without warning, my knees began to stiffen, forcing me to sit and rest. As soon as I did, I was overcome with exhaustion and my mind became clouded. Craig returned with a full container of fluid but my body had grown too weak to absorb much of it. We grew nervous. We risked missing the last bus from the trailhead to our car. It was nearing 5:00 P.M., and we had just arrived at the top of Nevada Falls. At the pace I was going, it would easily take another two hours to get to the trailhead. We were back at the slippery stone stairs, which were even more imposing going down. My right knee locked, requiring me to use Craig's shoulder as a crutch as I hobbled the final stretch. It was 6:55 P.M. The last bus was at 7:00. The final stretch was a long, straight path, ending at the trailhead. Though still a distance away, we could see the bus was there, ready to transport the last of the hikers. Craig sprinted ahead, and asked the bus driver to wait.

We got a lucky break. After the quick bus ride, we arrived at our car and I sat for a moment, desperately trying to gain my steadiness and get a second wind. I was hoping a little food and some water would do the trick. Craig was being positive, hoping for the same since our success surely called for a celebration. He had learned to read me well, and it was no secret that I was hurting more than I would admit. As we departed the parking lot, I turned to him and said, "Craig, I think I need to get checked out." I was feeling extremely weak and light-headed, and knew I needed some immediate medical attention. Within five minutes, we had arrived to Yosemite's Urgent Care Center.

Scared doesn't begin to define how I felt. I had grown accustomed to state-of-the-art medical facilities. The on-site medical clinic, while appropriate for a mountain environment, was equipped and staffed like a sick room in an elementary school. Furthermore, the medics were used to dealing with individuals who were fairly healthy, treating expected calamities such as dehydration, sprains, broken bones, and blisters. Given my medical history, my situation was anything but typical. In spite of the obvious symptom of severe dehydration, the attending doctor and nurse quickly decided the added challenge of my heart transplant was beyond their comfort level. In other words, they were more terrified of me than I was of them. To be on the safe side, they contacted the on-call doctor at UCLA, who instructed them to transfer me to a facility with appropriate resources. To do this, the doctor had to call Fresno, the nearest community with a sophisticated enough hospital, for transportation. While waiting for the ambulance to arrive, I was given an IV of saline fluid and Craig went to a nearby deli to buy me some soup. A blood test confirmed I was not only dehydrated, but my sodium levels were alarmingly depleted. The IV fluid would reverse the effects, but I needed calories as well. Soup was the ideal remedy. Fortunately, it was probably the only thing I could have kept down. As the hours ticked by, the salty fluid slowly helped me feel better.

Meanwhile, our friends, especially TJ, were growing increasingly worried. They'd expected us back for dinner. It was now past 9:00 P.M., darkness had fallen, and we had not returned. Adding to their fear, earlier in the day they'd seen a rescue helicopter making runs up the mountain around Half Dome. TJ's frayed nerves finally got the best of her. In an effort to locate us, she went to the sole phone booth outside of the group of cabins where we were staying. Following her intuition, her first call was to the Yosemite Urgent Care Clinic. Craig assured her I was fine. He said he would drive back to the cabin to pack up, and would inform everyone of the situation. As soon as Craig arrived, TJ took him aside for a private word. Clearly angry, she harshly scolded him, saying, "You would not have forgiven yourself if something happened to Kelly." Craig reassured her I was okay. They went back to the same phone booth and called me. Feeling defeated, I said to TJ, "If I ever say I want to climb another mountain, promise me you won't let me." As soon as the words escaped my lips, I regretted them. I knew they'd come back to haunt me.

It was after 11:00 P.M. I had been waiting nearly three hours for the ambulance to wind its way up to the Valley. Craig was back at the cabin gathering our belongings. As on previous trips, we brought a mountain of toys and gear —bikes, rafts, horseshoes, food, medical supplies and clothes—all of which Craig had to gather and load into the car. Just after 1:00 A.M., he started down the mountain. He was exhausted from a nineteen-hour day that had started at 5:00 A.M., included a thirteen-hour, seventeen-mile hike covering 4,100 vertical feet, and ended with a frightening medical emergency. An hour later, as Craig raced down the twisted mountain road while trying to stay awake, he saw an ambulance pulled over to the side. Figuring it had to be the one transporting me to Fresno, he nervously pulled in front and stopped the car. He approached the vehicle *and* tapped on the window. He asked, "Is there a Kelly Perkins inside?" The driver stared back at Craig with a look on his face that said; "Where in the hell did you come from, what are you doing on this road at 2:00 A.M., and how do you know the name of our patient?"

The driver answered with a hesitant "Yes."

Anxiously, Craig said, "I'm Kelly's husband. Is she okay?"

The driver looked back at the other EMT who was busily removing sheets, then peered at Craig and burst out laughing. "It depends," he finally said. "If you think wallowing in a bath of your own urine is fine then, yeah, she's okay." With all that IV fluid, I was desperate to pee, but failed miserably at handling the bedpan while careening down the curvy mountain road.

An hour later, I was admitted to St. Agnes Hospital in Fresno for severe dehydration (electrolyte imbalance). Craig managed two hours sleep in a stiff, plastic conference room chair by my side. Later that same morning, after several hours of IV fluid, a doctor looked at my heart rhythms and labs. He said, "Get out of here. Transplant patient or not, you are in better shape than me!"

I was discharged, and took with me a hugely valuable lesson. Thanks to a combination of errors—an undetected leak that left us with inadequate fluid, and lack of awareness of the diuretic effect of my medications—I'd been put at significant risk. I was determined it would never happen again.

In this, my first attempt after the transplant to "bag a peak," my goal had been to come down from the mountain stronger than ever. I wanted to prove to myself, and everyone else, that I was healthy again. I was not going to let fear of the unknown stand in my way. I didn't want to miss the opportunity to try to get back to something I really loved. But my troubled descent had the opposite effect. Craig was seen by some of our friends as careless, and I was judged as too frail to take such a risk. Yet, almost immediately, I felt compelled to choose an even larger mountain to climb. If Half Dome had not been such a harsh disappointment, maybe I wouldn't have felt so passionate about taking on an even bigger challenge. I have always had great respect for the majesty and power of mountains, but wasn't about to let myself be emotionally conquered by them.

Despite what could have been a disaster, Craig remained proud of my accomplishment, so much so that he contacted my hometown paper, the *Tahoe Daily Tribune*. He told them of my brave climb and my determination to reach the top, and they ran a lovely sort of "local girl does good" story. Craig figured it would be a nice, little article for my parents, who had been through so much with me, to share with their friends and neighbors. As it turned out, a talented Associated Press reporter named Brendan Riley, based in Carson City, noticed that tiny, local item. Himself an avid outdoorsman, he was so inspired by my conquest that he requested an interview and filed a feature story that was picked up throughout the western United States. That's when we first realized the power of sharing our success, especially for those desperately ill patients waiting for transplants as well as potential donors who are on the fence and have not yet made the decision to participate in the life-saving program.

CHAPTER 8

The Woman Who Danced with the Mountain

I RECALLED my rash promise to TJ that, after my Half Dome debacle, I was done with potentially risky climbs. Which is why, when I decided to attempt California's Mt. Whitney in 1997, I deliberately kept it a secret from her.

There were several symbolic reasons for choosing this mountain as my next conquest. First of all, it is the tallest mountain in the continental USA. Second, when I looked back at my climb to the top of it eleven years earlier, I considered it my greatest pre-transplant hiking accomplishment. I felt if I could repeat the feat, thereby reaching the summit with two different hearts, I could quell any naysayers who felt I was still too frail. Finally, at the time of that initial climb, Craig couldn't, due to altitude sickness, get past 13,600 feet and reach the top with me. Needless to say, standing together atop Mt. Whitney would be a significant milestone for us both.

Looking back, I realized I'd been emotionally ready to take on Half Dome, but my body had made it clear *it* wasn't ready. But, the Half Dome challenge did provide me with a little more information about my heart's capacity and my adrenaline endurance. Each time I pushed my personal limit, I was removing one more unknown.

The road back to the top began in January as I boosted my regular exercise program and began more rigorous training. My normal exercise regimen consisted of daily, three-mile walks in moderately hilly locations around our home. The training version upped the walk to four miles each weekday, augmented by longer (6- to 10-mile) weekend walks on steeper terrain. My strength varied from day to day, but by summer's end I felt a measurable increase in my endurance level.

Remembering what a grind Half Dome had been, I thought it would be smart to also join a gym in an effort to gain more muscle strength. There was a new all-women's facility close enough to our home that I could schedule my workout early, as soon as the gym opened at 5:30 A.M. This way, I could be first to use the machines and weights after the previous night's cleaning, enabling me to get a workout without exposing myself to the insipid viruses and bacteria that nest in such sweaty environments. I had another positive on my side. Since I had never weight trained seriously before, I didn't walk in with any expectations, which in my physical state might have zapped my spirit. I knew I would not be able to lift much, but my mind was set to show up and give it my best. I had come to learn that I couldn't significantly increase my heart strength or cardiac output, but I could compliment it by training my other muscles to help take the workload off my heart. This is precisely what I was after. Initially I liked the gym. I was there, without fail, five days a week. It was never a problem for me because I am a morning person and at my physical peak in the early hours. Also, that time of the morning corresponds with my "drug trough," when the medications in my body are at their lowest level and I feel nearly drug free.

To get started, I took advantage of my nutrition and science background, as well as three complimentary appointments with a personal trainer. To avoid injury, I began by learning the basic in-and-outs of the specific machines. In addition, I did homework—researching websites and pouring over magazines and books—all with the intent of mixing it up, adding variety and varying muscle groups on different days. My goal was to build strength in order to maximize my energy and endurance.

Before making the climb, Craig and I contacted Brendan, our new AP writer pal, who had asked if he could join us on our next major hike. After hearing our reasons for choosing Mt. Whitney, he felt a story would have a very positive impact on donor awareness. We welcomed the opportunity to share our experience.

My second recruit was my faithful walking partner, Susan, whose slow and deliberate steps made her the perfect pacesetter in Craig's absence. Although Susan had never backpacked in the mountains before, her adventurous spirit, coupled with her love of any fresh challenge, made her eager to join our team. And, recognizing the larger importance of our trek, she valued helping us reach our goals. My third enlistee was our amazingly strong and enthusiastic friend, Steve. His participation would help lighten my load, carrying enough water to make even a camel jealous. Rounding out the team was Maggie, Brendan's girlfriend. She was a courageous substitute, signing on just a week prior to our climb, as a last-minute replacement for a participant who had sustained an injury.

A month before our scheduled departure, we had a preliminary get together with our local team members to

Kelly, Craig and Art Nelson with Skis on backpack trip, Lake Aloha, Tahoe, California. 1983.

Desolation Wilderness, Lake Tahoe, third annual backpack trip with college friends, left to right: TJ Hagen (Nelson), Brian Paulsen, Craig, Kelly, Jeff Nelson, Kelly Toohey (McGovern), Mark McGovern, and Art Nelson. 1985.

Kelly and Craig hiking in Zermatt, Switzerland, in the shadow of the Matterhorn, just prior to first symptoms of illness. May 1992.

Kelly's thirty-first birthday during her first month in the hospital at at Good Samaritan, Los Angeles. September 1992.

Kelly with her Mom, Dad, and Craig at first dinner out after her transplant, Walnut Creek, California. 1996.

Kelly ascending the famous cables on Half Dome just 10 months after her heart transplant, Yosemite, California. 1996.

Craig and Kelly peering over the edge on top of Half Dome, a photo that was made into their 1996 Christmas card. 1996.

Craig and Kelly blow bubbles in celebration of reaching the 14,496-foot summit of Mt. Whitney, California. 1997.

"I'm Back!" Craig holds Kelly after completion of the Mt. Whitney trek, a milestone after reaching the summit with two different hearts. 1997.

Craig reading a letter from the daughter of Kelly's donor. Mt. Fuji, Japan, 1998.

Kelly & Craig releasing donor's ashes atop Mt. Fuji. 1998.

Kelly and Craig speaking at Amercian Heart Association function, Newport Beach, California. 2000.

Kelly and Susan Kjesbo share a hug at 15,000 feet, exceeding her previous altitude high, a milestone for a heart transplant recipient at that time. 2001.

Expedition team members supporting Mt. Kilimanjaro trek, base camp at 15,000 feet. 2001.

Kelly signing in at the Groote Schuur Transplant Museum in South Africa. Painting of Dr. Christiaan Barnard, first doctor to perform a heart transplant, in the background. 2001.

Kelly on rappel, Dri Hornli Ridge, Saas Fe, Switzerland. 2003.

Kelly on Dri-Hornli Ridge, Saas Fe, Switzerland, with Craig in background. 2003.

Matterhorn team, left to right: Michael Brown, Cedric Zulauff, Craig, Kelly, Jean Pavillard, and Tim Brown. 2003.

Kelly and Craig on top of Mt. Rolling Pin in Mount Aspiring National Park, New Zealand. 2005.

Nick, Kelly, and Craig ascending a ridge during their climb in Mt. Aspiring National Park, New Zealand. 2005.

"Our inspiration." A natural heart feature on the Southwest face of El Capitan, Yosemite.

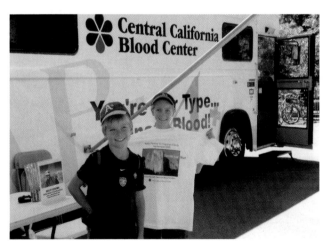

"Exercise Your Heart" Blood Drive during Kelly's El Capitan climb; Grady and Casey Nelson in front of blood mobile. 2005.

Kelly on Muir Wall, El Capitan, Yosemite, California. 2005.

Kelly and Craig on a portaledge, Muir Wall, El Capitan, Yosemite, California. 2005.

Scott Stowe with our team below on Muir Wall, El Capitan, Yosemite, California. 2005.

Kelly signing autographs at the Explorer's Film Festival, Lodz, Poland. 2005.

Craig and Kelly at a University of San Francisco fundraising event, Los Angeles, California. 2006.

discuss some of the basics. Craig had gathered details about the Mt. Whitney trail and the campsites we would be staying at, along with specifics about camping, gear, first aid, weather, altitude sickness, food, my medical condition and, just for safekeeping, detailed directions to the nearest hospital. It was an informative meeting, leaving everyone fully aware of what we were getting into and prepared for the challenge that lay ahead. Craig and I always have said that a successful trip is one that is well planned. After the Half Dome experience, it was a point we couldn't stress enough.

As our departure date neared, guilt began chipping away at my excitement. Eventually, I knew, TJ would find out. I had been a coward, afraid of what she would say. Knowing that Brendan's story would likely surface in newspapers, I needed to tell her the truth, and do so before the climb. I plucked up my courage, and made the call. As expected, she was not happy, but not shocked.

Later she sent me a letter, recapping our earlier discussion. She wrote:

> *After talking to you at the medical unit in Yosemite, when you were so scared, and not yet sure if your problem was just dehydration, I really thought that scare would have squashed the urge for you to hike again. I don't know if you remember Kelly, but you did say to me, "I never need to hike another mountain again." You know, the same gusto that has enabled you to overcome great physical challenges has also been your foe—you can go too far. Remember the excessive marathon training just prior to your wedding? Of course I am going to worry. Knowing how you have pushed yourself beyond your physical limits at different times in your life, I was very worried*

*about your ability to properly judge if you were ready
for the Half Dome hike. I know you, and know that
if you're caught in a 50/50 situation, that you'd
rather take the risk than abort the challenge. Craig
has the same drive. I don't mean that I thought you
weren't being careful, or taking necessary precautions,
but we can all be cautious and yet the unexpected can
happen. I also didn't think that you were quite strong
enough, and that maybe you hadn't been medically
stable long enough. It's not that I thought you couldn't
make it, but you were still very thin, and without a
lot of reserved energy. I just felt like the risk was too
great. After all you'd been through, coming so very
close to dying, it didn't seem like a hike should be so
important. Of course the real fear for me was that
this hike could cause me to lose my friend, and I just
couldn't comprehend your need or desire to do it.*

I was touched that she cared so much, but wanted her
to understand my need to validate my health and refocus
my energy. Ultimately, she did come around, though her
blessing was guarded at best. I was relieved she now knew
and pleased to have her support, even if tentative.

Many healthy people can hike Whitney in two days.
Some even manage to go up and down the same day. We
took three days. We wanted to make it to the summit and
back safely. Thousands of climbers get permits each year
and many are forced to turn back because of the altitude,
just as Craig had more than a decade earlier. To help
ensure our success, Craig, Susan, and I added three days
on the front end of the trip, to sleep and day hike in a
higher elevation, further helping our bodies to acclimatize.
I had enough issues, and given Craig's history, we didn't
want to add altitude sickness to our list of concerns.

An area "test" hike we made near the Whitney trailhead proved extremely informative. I paid attention to my vitals, just as the doctors did in the hospital, monitoring my blood pressure, heart rate, and ease or difficulty of breathing. I felt so free, so exhilarated about attempting our upcoming Whitney assault, yet a bit fearful of pushing my limits. I grew confident I could make it to the top, but remained concerned about making it back down. Interestingly enough, both Susan and Craig had headaches at the 10,000-foot level during the preparation hike, while I felt fine. Craig and I both wore heart rate monitors for comparative purposes. The difference was apparent. My heart rate increased more slowly and seemed to cap at around 130 bpm, higher than I had been able to get it at sea level. Naturally, Craig's was normal, and continued to rise with his increased oxygen demands, escalating from 130 to 150. The same was true, in reverse, whenever we rested. His would return quickly to normal, while we waited for my heart to figure out I had stopped and was no longer exerting myself.

The remainder of the team arrived the evening before we began our Mt. Whitney ascent. The next morning we all rallied, well rested, ate breakfast, and loaded our backpacks for the three-day and two-night roundtrip event. After several rounds of loading, unloading, and reloading, each of us found a weight our bodies could handle, and we started off on the trail. The first mile was brutal as my body grudgingly adjusted to the added pounds I was carrying. As the weight settled, my backpack slowly digging its way into my bony shoulders and hips, I was able to focus on more pressing issues, such as breathing. Knowing my pack was the lightest of the group, I was not about to complain.

Susan assumed her usual role, setting a slow pace that I could manage. Around 1:00 P.M., we stopped off at Lone

Pine Lake, ate lunch, and rested in the warm sun. There is a spectacular view from the lakeshore, down to the valley floor through a perfect V-shape, surrounded by towering peaks reaching to the sky above. The stunning natural beauty was as nourishing as our food and water. We continued on to our campsite, Outpost Camp, which was just over 10,000 feet in elevation. As we set up our tents, Craig took off to the nearby stream to double purify enough water to sustain us through the evening and much of the next day. While most people simply purify water once, given my immunosuppressive state, we took extra precaution. The last thing I wanted was to pick up some microscopic bacteria or parasite that would find my body the perfect place to call home.

The next day was going to be a big one, and we all wanted to preserve our energy for the grueling fourteen-mile trek that was going to take us skyward some 4,000 feet, to a head-pounding elevation of 14,496 feet above sea level. Most of the incline, about 3,500 feet, is gained in the first five miles, meaning extremely steep switchbacks!

That night, I got a bit of a scare. My stomach began to ache and I got a slight case of diarrhea. My main concern was that I was becoming dehydrated. Since I knew from my Half Dome experience that these symptoms could be quite serious, Craig and I made silent plans to go back down the mountain in the morning if my discomfort continued. I was heartbroken, but tried to remain strong. I had trained and planned for this trip for so long. Still, I had to keep things in perspective. I had struggled too long with my illness to put myself in jeopardy. Fortunately, I remained stable throughout the night, so we made the decision to continue on.

After the break of dawn, I cautiously set out on my quest to become the first person to reach the summit with two separate hearts. Craig, Susan, Brendan, Maggie, and Steve carried their own packs and shared the weight of my supplies, which included my blood pressure machine, medications, oxygen, water purifier, cell phone, water, food, and foul weather clothes. It was clearly a gallant team effort to increase my chances of reaching the top.

We left the camp around 7:00 A.M. After a grueling morning of nonstop hiking, we reached Trail Camp, elevation 12,039 feet, where we stopped to purify more water and fill up for the final ascent.

The pace slowed, but we continued to move ahead, taking it one step at a time. At approximately 13,600 feet we reached the ridge of Trail Crest. Here, Craig and I shared a celebratory kiss in honor of him reaching his previous high point. I recalled from the prior ascent that the remaining two miles were quick. Unfortunately, my memory was a little faulty. At 2:30 P.M., after what seemed an eternity, we all gathered under a spectacular blue sky to simultaneously walk the final steps to the geographical marker identifying the summit, the highest point on the continental United States.

Tears rolled down our faces. Everyone knew how much this accomplishment meant to me. I had made it to the peak, this time with a second heart *and* my husband. I truly felt on top of the world. I raised my hands in victory and cried out to Craig, "We did it!"

As I shared congratulatory hugs with the team, Craig scurried off to dig into his backpack, revealing several commemorative surprises. First he presented me with a golden replica of Mt. Whitney, instantly doubling the number of mountain charms on my bracelet. It was beautifully handcrafted, detailing each jagged feature of the popular mountain. Next, in fond remembrance of the tradition shared with us by the bubble ladies on Half

Dome was a bundle of wish wands. Each wand came with a corresponding letter spelling out a specific wish for me, from family, friends, and medical professionals who had cheered me on from the sidelines. All the letters were uplifting, offering heartfelt praise. One was from Dr. Cannom. Thanks to him, I was able to overcome numerous difficult medical challenges, and it was with overwhelming emotion that I read of his continued support, knowing he was still keeping an eye on me.

The trek back to Outpost Camp was pleasantly uneventful, making for a successful twelve-hour roundtrip day. The only significant hiccup was with Brendan, who had blood pressure issues of his own, forcing him to lag behind in both the final ascent and descent. In fact, well after we got to camp, darkness having fallen, Brendan and Maggie still hadn't arrived. Concerned for their welfare, Craig geared up with headlamps and extra water to begin the trek back up in search of them. I was physically exhausted and couldn't fathom starting that hike again. Fortunately Craig didn't have to hike too high before he spotted them on the trail, armed with only a tiny penlight as they struggled to make their way through the pitch-black night. We'd all made it back safe and planned, after a well-earned sleep, to head down to our cars first thing in the morning.

The final day was easygoing, and I was still on a tremendous high! Upon reaching the bottom, Craig lifted me up in his arms in celebration of a mission accomplished. My image was forever changed. I was back!

Brendan wrote a wonderful article that was picked up worldwide. Based on the emails we received, we felt our adventurous tale had a most positive impact on organ donation awareness. We were also able to share our experiences with several TV stations, intrigued by the warm "human interest" aspect of this unusual feat. For us, it was another way to spread the word on organ donation, so we were more than willing to make ourselves available. With all this goodwill, it was also our first exposure to the media's more exploitative side. One call came to Craig from a producer at *Dateline*, who recognized the sweetness of our story. But, when the producer pitched the story to his executive committee, they decided to pass, claiming it wasn't "tragic enough." Craig's response: "If tragedy is what you are looking for, we hope we are never candidates for your program."

While *Dateline* may have wanted tragedy, others heartily applauded our efforts. One of the emails we received was from a young woman who had taken a picture with us atop the mountain. She wrote:

> *Dear Kelly,*
>
> *I was so inspired by meeting you at the top of Mt. Whitney. We took a picture of you and your group, and ironically, I was so excited for you that I forgot to have my own picture taken at the top. I had a pretty serious case of mountain sickness, but the misery subsided for a short while and the endorphins kicked in when I realized what an accomplishment you made. Basically, I was humbled. I had spent the morning whining and moaning about the nausea, dizziness, headache and every other symptom I could grasp. Bleck! You have made this whole trip worth it. I will always think of you as the woman who danced with the mountain.*

CHAPTER 9

Release

A YOUNG Japanese girl named Miyuki Monobe arrived in the United States for a heart transplant. Her unusual story captured Craig's and my full attention, leaving us to ponder why she had to travel all the way from Japan for the surgery. We came to learn that the law in Japan recognized death as occurring only after the heart stopped beating (which is too late for the organ to be recovered for transplantation.) In a strange example of synchronicity, the article about Miyuki had appeared in a March 1997 newspaper, on the same page as a follow-up story about our climb up Half Dome. Miyuki subsequently died fifteen days later, leaving a profound effect on us. We empathized deeply with the suffering her family endured, imagining their tortuous struggle to reconcile Japan's archaic laws with their daughter's tragically unnecessary death.

Miyuki's death pointed us to our next climb. The Japanese finally passed a new law that recognized brain death, which in turn paved the way for heart transplants. To celebrate, Craig and I decided to climb Japan's most famous cultural symbol—the sacred Mt. Fuji. Our goal was to heighten awareness of this meaningful advancement and the important shift in perception about organ donation that it would ignite among the Japanese people. Changing a law was one thing, but changing an entire culture's perspective was a much bigger challenge. Speaking of cultural shifts, women weren't even allowed to climb Mt. Fuji until the nineteenth century! Only with the slow but steady march of small steps can deep-rooted beliefs give way to liberating modern ideas and understandings. We wanted to be one of the sparks that ignited such liberation, and hoped our climb would inspire the Japanese people to begin discussing the issue.

After conquering Mt. Whitney, and in celebration of my good health, I joined my parents on a trip to Italy. Although Craig couldn't go with us, due to his need to catch up on work, it turned out to be a unique and rare opportunity for me to reconnect with my mom and dad in a culture that prided itself on ease. Laid-back Italy was certainly a far cry from the medical stress we'd all been immersed in for so long! One evening while I was away, Craig arrived home from work, tossed his briefcase on the table, fell exhausted into a chair and hit the play button on the answering machine. What he heard was startling: "Hi! I hope this is the right Kelly Perkins. My name is Greta. This call may sound strange, but I think you have my mother's heart."

Craig leapt to his feet, hit repeat, and listened more closely. A chill raced up his spine as he contemplated these shocking words. He wrote down her number. Because the area code indicated she lived back east, he figured it was too late to return the call. He then wrestled over whether to wait until I returned from Europe or make the call himself. Since I wasn't due home for another week, he decided to go ahead and at least acknowledge we'd received the message. The next morning, he made two attempts to reach Greta, but got her machine both times. Though he was reluctant, given the sensitive nature of the call, to use voicemail, when there was no answer a third time, he did leave a message stating that, yes, she had reached the right Kelly.

Greta, sounding young and shy, her voice quivering, called back the next day.

Sensing her nervousness, Craig gently took control of the conversation. He set her at ease by thanking her for making contact and letting her know I was doing well. He then explained that I was currently traveling, but would be eager to speak with her as soon as I returned. He continued to fill the silence by trying to express the inexpressible: how profoundly grateful we were for her family's decision to donate her mother's organs.

After a lengthy pause, Greta finally spoke: "My grandmother saw a story about Kelly in a local newspaper," she began. "She called me immediately. It happened to be my birthday," she nervously confided. "We saw right away that there were too many coincidences; I just knew Kelly had my mom's heart." Pausing again to compose herself, she continued, "My mom was forty years old, and ever so healthy and athletic. She was living temporarily in California. The accident was just that, an accident. She was out riding and the horse threw her. I flew out to be with her in the hospital, fully expecting her to recover, but . . . it just happened. A blood clot."

After he hung up the phone, Craig contemplated how best to inform me of this unexpected development. Respecting my sensitivity and prior expressed apprehension regarding contact with my donor's family, and given his knack for making things special, he wanted to wait and find the perfect time and place.

Meanwhile, surrounded by the ruins of Rome's glorious past, I called to tell him I loved him and find out if anything was new at home. "As a matter of fact, yes!" said

Craig. "Some very exciting news. You were contacted by *Good Morning America*. They're interested in you sharing your story about the recent climb up Mt. Whitney. In fact, they would like us to be at their sister studio in Oakland for a live interview the day after you return."

We determined the logistics would work well. I wanted to be on the same return flight as my parents, so I was landing in San Francisco, which made the time and location for the interview convenient. The opportunity to share our adventure meant everything to me, primarily because there are far too few positive stories on organ donation.

Craig knew the real secret had to wait. At the airport, he stood just outside the gate for me, like a dutiful valet driver, holding a sign plastered with two big hearts. Despite my bone-numbing exhaustion from the long flight, the sight of him sent a heart-pounding thrill right through me. After talking his ears off about our adventures, I was too wound up to get to sleep. But, knowing we had a 4:00 A.M. pickup for the interview, I gave it my best effort. No sooner had my eyes finally shut, than the alarm clock started buzzing. We dashed to the studio, where we were ushered inside a closet-sized room packed with AV equipment, cameras, and monitors against an otherwise blank wall. With nothing other than Charlie Gibson's voice pouring into our earpieces, we were finally given the cue we were on live. Jet lag and sleeplessness enabled me to look the part—close to death, which is how many people imagine heart transplant recipients. If the interview weren't difficult enough, conversing with a camera lens that you're supposed to believe is one of America's foremost TV personalities, made it tough for me to show any genuine emotion or be animated in any way. Craig, on the other hand, talked to the camera as though it was his best friend. At least one of us was "on"!

Suddenly, Charlie made an interesting remark, "I suspect when you got to the top there was a thought and a word for your donor." Though it was a reasonable observation, I felt caught off guard, perhaps not wanting to engage in a dialog about my specific donor or her family. I sputtered and said, "Oh, you bet. I mean, I thank my donor every day. And, um, I, oh, certainly . . . I thought of the donor all the way up. I really did. I do daily." As I proceeded along my tongue-tripping path, Craig looked at me with affectionate pride; but he must have been twisting inside thinking, "you're about to have more than just a few thoughts and words for your donor."

Anxious to quickly shift the focus from my donor to the more universal issue, I went on to say, "One message I would like to get out to people is, for all those families who have donated family organs, I just want to say thank you, and look what it has done for me. And if you have any questions about signing a donor card, please do so." Having stumbled through the interview I was determined to get my important message out. My intended words were cut short, but I made it just under the wire. The music swelled, indicating it was time for a commercial, at the exact moment I uttered the final word of my coast-to-coast donor plea.

A few days after returning to Southern California, Craig suggested we go for a hike to Crystal Cove in scenic Laguna Beach, a place we often visited, and where we trained for Half Dome and Mt. Whitney. Accessed by steep, hilly trails perched above the Pacific Ocean, it ranks among nearby wilderness areas as one of our favorites. After a spring rain, low-lying brush paints the land a rich, emerald green. As we crested the ridge, Craig guided me to the place that marked the first, tiny peak I'd conquered after my transplant.

He sat me down and said he had something to tell me. He pulled a piece of paper from his pocket and began to explain its significance. Staring down at the scribbled phone number, Craig recapped Greta's heart-warming call. He told me how she had managed to convey the emotional loss caused by her mother's death, how that loss was softened by the joy of learning that her mom's heart now beat inside someone else, and how grateful she was that it was me.

My eyes flooded with tears. Any fear of personalizing my new heart immediately faded. This young girl's tremendous emotional strength in the face of such personal tragedy touched me deeply and forever. Something strange happened, something best described as the legacy of Eve. Curiosity overwhelmed me. As much as I'd believed I didn't want to know, I suddenly had umpteen questions about my donor. Where was she from? Was she happily married? Was Greta able to say good-bye to her?

Craig shared the few details he knew, including one special coincidence. Her name was Carol—the same as my mother. So, two Carols had given me life. Carol, my savior, began to loom large in my mind. I spent the day in an acute state of sadness for the very reason I had previously avoided any donor information—because now she was so real, so loved, and so missed.

Greta told Craig that the Crystal Cove area of Laguna Beach was a favorite place of her mom's as well. How strange and magical! Carol was originally from back East and yet she stumbled upon this very same place, and had come to cherish it as much as we did. Serendipitously, while I went there to rebuild my physical self, she may have chosen it as the place to rebuild her spiritual self.

Regardless, we were both responding to a calling. I embraced it as fate.

A few months later, while preparing for the Mt. Fuji hike and unbeknownst to me, Craig decided to contact Greta and my donor's sister, Nancy, to request that they participate in our newly adopted bubble-blowing tradition. He asked that they send a special wish along with a bubble wand, which I could carry to the top of Mt. Fuji. Greta and Nancy were delighted to comply. Then, Greta had a very special request of her own. "I have my mom's ashes. Would you and Kelly be willing to release them from the top of Mt. Fuji? It would be such an honor to her memory. If you don't feel comfortable, please just say so."

Craig didn't hesitate, responding with an immediate and powerful "yes." Still, this was a huge request. He hung up the phone and immediately began to consider how emotionally overwhelming it might be for me. He especially didn't want me to feel any added pressure about making it to the mountaintop. He decided to keep it a secret until we'd reached the summit.

While Craig was worried about how to present me with the ashes when we completed our ascent, there was a more immediate concern: how was he going to keep me from picking up the mail and opening the package? Also, was it legal to go through customs with ashes? And was it legal to release ashes atop Mt. Fuji, or in Japan at all? Does Japanese law prohibit it? For a moment, he imagined a beautiful tribute to my donor being followed by a police escort down the mountain and a post-climb victory party inside a jail cell!

Craig placed a flurry of calls to U.S. customs, the Japanese Consulate, and even funeral homes, but got conflicting answers to these crucial questions. Some said absolutely not, others said they didn't know, but never did he hear a reassuring "yes." So, risking potentially criminal behavior, Craig decided to just do it. He spoke to Susan, who had accepted our invitation to come along on the trip for added safety, just as she'd done on Mt. Whitney. "I'll pack the ashes," she graciously offered. "That way Kelly won't see them in your suitcase should you be searched at the airport." Though Craig worried about any legal hassles Susan might face at customs, he agreed it was the safest solution. Looking back, I remember how goofy Susan and Craig were acting after they passed through airport security. Now I understand—it wasn't silliness, but rather relief!

On July 9, 1998, we began our 12,380-foot ascent. Mt. Fuji is one of the most recognized and visually pleasing shapes in the world. The perfect volcanic-cone symmetry juts boldly skyward, resembling an inverted fan. The peak is an aggregate volcano, building over time as layer upon layer of lava and ash is added to its slopes.

Like its magnificent geological evolution, Mount Fuji's symbolic history has also developed over time. Changing beliefs have added new meaning. Within Japan's two most prominent religions, Shinto and Buddhism, Mt. Fuji is thought to have sacred power. Since the sixth century, it has been a pilgrimage for people from all corners of the globe. Climbing the mountain has become a metaphor for the ascent to spiritual enlightenment. Numerous shrines and temples surround the base, the slopes and the top. Japanese worshipers, who are unable to make the inspirational trek, use lava sand from the mountain to create a miniature Fuji in their home garden or shrine. This climb is not to be underestimated. A famous proverb says, "He who climbs Mt. Fuji once is a wise man, he who climbs it twice is a fool."

We were hiking on hallowed ground, following in the footsteps of millions who had made the pilgrimage before us. We couldn't understand the language of the signs, but didn't need too. We immediately felt a deep connection to the mountain's profound power.

I was so thrilled about finally beginning this journey, my heart fluttered with excitement. But experience had taught me that I needed to pace myself, or else the steep trail would too quickly reveal my limitations. Making our way to the Eighth Station, the final destination before the sunrise ascent, we took a breather at each of the huts along the trail. The stops provided precisely the reprieve I needed both physically and mentally. While my body caught its breath, my mind was reinvigorated with my purpose for being there.

We arrived at the Eighth Station hut by early evening. The tiny interior was constructed entirely of wood, with floors, walls, and ceilings all embellished with Japanese prayer flags. Spotlessly clean and neatly organized, it came complete with a prepackaged curry-and-rice dinner and hot morning meal. Off the main dining area were two rooms lined with wooden platform shelves for sleeping. We spread our blankets and attempted to get a few hours shuteye before departing for the summit at midnight.

Near the door, we found an unclaimed area on a lower bunk big enough to accommodate our entire team. Thinking safety first and wanting to stay healthy, I positioned myself between Susan and Craig—psychologically creating my germ-free bubble—and tried to rest. It was crowded and, though the room was designated as a quiet area, extremely noisy—not with chattering but with loud snores from exhausted climbers.

Sleep eluded me. The culprit? Sleeping ten feet away, a large man had blissfully surrendered to the deepest sleep of his life, snoring like an overweight asthmatic in a smoke-filled room. Drawing upon every mental trick I knew, I struggled to shut him out, but no luck. After an hour of tossing and turning, my anxiety steadily mounting, I leapt up and asked our Japanese guide, Asano, to interpret my request for the man to be quiet. As annoyed as I was, I realized the poor, tired soul had no idea the misery he was causing everyone else. But Asano wasn't about to play intermediary. "Go. *You* wake him," she insisted. By this point, my frustration had built to a dark peak. No way was I going to let this guy unwittingly compromise my journey before it had even begun.

"Okay," I said to Asano, "I will." I stepped to the floor, walked over to the man's bunk and tapped his arm. He woke with alarm, and his kind, soft eyes locked with mine. Knowing it was highly unlikely he could speak any English, I raised my index finger to my lips and gave the universal signal for "Shush!" He blinked back at me with utter incomprehension. I suddenly saw myself through his perplexed gaze: a small, angry American woman hovering above him in the dark of night, shaking a finger for no reason he could comprehend.

Embarrassed, even mortified, I caught the eye of a man on the bunk above him who had watched the entire incident. He had been meditating in the lotus position. Until, of course, I distracted him! I was expecting to be punished with a searing look. Instead, much to my surprise, he smiled and giggled. That tiny wave of laughter was as soothing and reinvigorating as an eight-hour sleep.

At the stroke of midnight, July 10, we exited the mountain hut to begin our final ascent to Mt. Fuji's peak. Our unwavering focus stayed on my health and strength. Craig watched me closely, secretly wondering if I had adequate energy to reach the top. Also, mindful of his own susceptibility to the thin air, he was as determined to pace himself as he was to pace me.

The hike was very steep, with short switchbacks and lots of loose gravel rocks. We had reason to be concerned. I had just been weaned off one of my major drugs, a steroid, which had been causing my muscles to cramp and fatigue. Emotionally and mentally, I had been tapped dry. This was new territory for me. My body had always relied on my mental strength to bridge the gap. As we started off, the night sky revealed a scattering of stars, the full moon shining bright and strong. The moonlight was augmented by our headlamps as we negotiated our way through the cracks in the frozen lava. Midway up the final leg, I began to take frequent rest stops. My breathing became labored and fatigue was setting in fast. The curry dinner sat uncomfortably in my stomach. That, and my lack of sleep, added to the extreme challenge of the hike.

Since safety always came first, Craig's plans for divulging his special secret were now in limbo. After each rest, I was able to rally and resume my pace, but my energy level was getting dicey. Still, I was determined to reach the top.

After four-and-a-half hours of hiking in the middle of the night on steep, jagged terrain, we neared the top of Mt. Fuji. It is often referred to as the place where heaven meets earth. After a final set of stairs, the trail led us under a tall wooden "tori" gate. Legends tell of enfeebled climbers using the sturdy beams as anchors to prevent being blown thousands of feet down by the fierce winds at the summit. As my tired body was whipped by the growing wind, I could identify with each and every one of them. The final leg leads to a commemorative shrine and mountain hut nestled close to the rim of the crater. Adding to its mysteriousness, a veil of thick fog and wind-whipped mist had moved in and shrouded the peak.

I had made it! And Craig had made it!

Tears of joy filled my eyes as we settled into a small corner of the mountaintop hut. Craig immediately found some hot soup to help me refuel. My cheeks flushed as I slowly warmed up and regained my energy. I commented to Craig and our team, "This hike had been a slog, much more challenging than expected."

I was thrilled to be inside, sheltered from the wind and cold. The minimalist hut had just a concrete floor and wooden benches, but the body heat of the climbers warmed it. In addition to our friend Susan and guide Asano, our intimate little celebration included Junji and Eric, a photographer and a writer from the Associated Press. After a few moments of warming up and regaining circulation to my toes and fingers, Craig presented me with a charm of Mt. Fuji for my bracelet. Frankly, I sort of secretly expected it. Still, knowing it might be coming never took away from the excitement of actually receiving it, or more importantly, what it meant to achieve another success. This latest addition was a cone-shaped yellow-gold replica accented with a white-gold cap. It was stunning, and I knew it would instantly bring me right back to this mystical spot every time I looked at it.

Time for bubbles! We put on our layers of gear and ventured back outside, where the wind still howled. Craig positioned me atop the shrine's steps while trying to protect me from the worst of the blustery weather. He took out our bottle of bubbles and placed the suds-soaked wand next to my mouth. Just as I was about to blow, a strong gust did the job for me, and a stream of bubbles floated off.

Craig gently squeezed my hand and said, "I have another surprise for you." Susan and the rest of our team stepped back, recognizing our need for a private moment. Having employed such imagination and taken so many risks to bring his secret to the summit, Craig tenderly began to share his clandestine mission. He explained how he was in contact with the donor's family, had requested a special wish from them, and what they had asked in return.

With prayers, wishes, and bubbles still soaring above, Craig pulled from his camera bag a neatly folded letter and a small leather pouch about the size and shape of a human heart. As I held my breath, he began to read Greta's carefully crafted words. My heart began to race. As if passing a torch, Craig placed in my hands the remains of a life that now beat within me. Our strenuous hike seemed inconsequential in comparison to the magnitude of the moment. I was happy, sad, depleted, confused. My emotional barrel was simply overflowing. Craig recognized the drain, but also knew the importance of fulfilling the donor family's wishes. The moving tribute was not yet complete.

Craig knew I had chosen to preserve my donor's anonymity and wouldn't want to see her photo. But, in addition to Greta's letter and the remarkable request concerning her mom's ashes, Nancy had supplied an 8 x 10 close-up of Carol, her beloved sister. Craig knew that, in order to share her photo with me, he would need to someway minimize its impact. Putting his imagination to use yet again, he not only reduced the picture to fit on a wallet-sized card, but also modified the image into a very soft transparency. She looked like a distant angel. Further protecting me from my donor's reality, Craig superimposed text from a prayer that had been read at her memorial service over the softened photo. A sobering thought ran through my mind. Her heart had been beating inside me during her funeral. I was truly overcome with emotion as I looked at the face of my heart.

Craig then guided me over to the summit's edge, where we sat down and read the prayer. As we released Carol's ashes, the wind roared off the ridge as if it were anxiously waiting to carry them away. For an instant, the clouds parted and we could see the sunlight breaking, shining all the way down to the valley below. We sat motionless as the ashes spiraled into the air like wild birds taking flight. At that moment, I felt my new heart truly became mine.

CHAPTER 10

Dog Years

OUR climb up Mt. Fuji was truly beautiful and symbolic. In recognition of its personal theme, Craig kept the news that he was carrying Carol's ashes as much a secret from me as he did from Eric and Junji. In fact, it wasn't until five minutes before he revealed the secret that he told our AP companions, doing so only because he wanted them to step back and provide us some private space to share the precious moment. They knew they were witnessing something very special. When the reporters subsequently informed their editors that they were delivering an exceptional human-interest story of significant cultural importance, the bureau chief decided to hold the article for a feature release. Providing a shot in the arm for organ donation, the story was picked up and embraced by news publications around the world. Beautifully conveying the message we wanted to get out, that the *real* hero was inside of me, its impact was humbling, exceeding all our expectations.

We had no climbs planned for the balance of the year, but continued to "experience" all we could. Since the earliest days of our marriage, Craig and I have maintained a tradition regarding the celebration of both Valentines Day and our anniversary. Each year we trade off, with one of us planning something special to commemorate both occasions. This year was Craig's turn, and he surprised me by fulfilling a dream I'd shared with him when we first starting dating. I'd grown up skiing in the mountains, but hadn't been on skis since 1992, just before my illness. So, Craig decided that we would spend Valentines Day in Telluride, one of Colorado's most magnificent winter resorts. Soon after we arrived, we saw a helicopter land adjacent to the hotel and learned it belonged to a heli-ski firm that offered day trips to various backcountry mountains. I jumped at the opportunity. My first time back on skis was going to be more adventurous than I had ever imagined. And, this adventure was sure to be a vast improvement over my last helicopter experience—aboard the air ambulance! We would be skiing in untracked powder, on some of the highest helicopter-access terrain in the world. It was a thrilling experience, lifting up off the snow, flying over the village to the San Juan Mountains, home to the greatest concentration of 13,000-foot and 14,000-foot peaks south of the Canadian Yukon. I had my typical cold feet, but not from nerves, even when the pilot augmented his safety instructions with a graphic description of his recent helicopter crash in the very same area. But I wasn't about to be spooked. The excitement of it all was too overwhelming to be spoiled by "what ifs." I adopted a "que sera sera" attitude. My new philosophy was "life is *now*." The helicopter dropped us off and we hunkered down as it lifted off, leaving us in sweeping surroundings of snow-covered peaks. My adrenaline was at an all-time high, and it took no time at all to regain my long-dormant skiing skills. I rejoiced in the freedom of space the vast, snow-blanketed mountains provided. To me, this was heaven on earth! As lunchtime approached, Craig began feeling off-kilter. We'd just completed our second drop off on one of the higher peaks, when he became so overheated he thought he was going to internally combust. Slowly making his way down the powdery slopes, he began to sweat profusely. The rapid purge of fluids left him damp and clammy. The onset was so quick he had no headache, typically the first sign of altitude sickness. Instead, he became extremely nauseous and began vomiting. His symptoms were all too familiar to me. He had to be airlifted off the mountain, taken to the clinic, and treated with IV fluids. A perfect morning was clouded by a very scary afternoon. Yet, ever the trooper, Craig managed to rally for a romantic Valentine's Day dinner.

As thrilling as our ski trip was, it couldn't compare to the exciting news awaiting us when we returned home. It was February 28 and, for the first time in three decades, a heart transplant had been performed in Japan. Bolstered by such a thrilling breakthrough, we knew our future course was set. We would travel the world, using our adventurous lifestyle to generate ever-greater awareness of the life-saving importance of organ donation.

The tale of our Mt. Fuji climb found another, rather intriguing outlet—one that, quite literally, got Craig in the *Soup*. During my weeks and months of hospitalization, Craig had purchased several volumes from Jack Canfield's bestselling series of *Chicken Soup for the Soul* books. During especially grim times, when we seemed to be drowning in pessimism, we'd often turn to them, randomly selecting a passage and finding it an ideal antidote for rekindling my broken spirit. Much to our surprise and delight, Craig was contacted by the series' editors and asked to write a piece about our Mt. Fuji experience for their next book, *Chicken Soup for the Traveler's Soul*. Given the series' enormous popularity, Craig's lovingly crafted contribution added significantly to our ongoing awareness campaign.

Despite our eagerness to be ambassadors for organ donation, Craig and I really needed to get our relationship, our careers, and our finances back on track. My illness and recovery had been all consuming. Every other aspect our lives had, by necessity, taken a back seat. Dealing with a single issue, even one as large and threatening as my precarious health, was easier than coping with the myriad of smaller concerns that now descended. Our lives were broken, and we needed to fit unfamiliar pieces back together, making the puzzle whole again. One thing we knew for sure: having children was no longer a consideration. The physical risk was too great, and there was the ever-looming possibility that, even if I survived childbirth, my health could, at any point, take a rapid, downward spiral. So, we accepted that our family would remain just the two of us. Luckily our good friends shared their familial wealth. TJ's daughter Casey was our first godchild. Jake, Mark's son, became our second.

High atop our priority list was rebuilding our relationship, restoring the balance that had always defined it. I used to be very shy and demurely patient, anxious to avoid any type of confrontation. Craig was the opposite, an extravert who was very social, outgoing, and did not hesitate to speak his mind. We respected and embraced our differences, and considered ourselves absolute equals. Then, during and after my illness, the balance shifted. I was too scared, too drugged, or too preoccupied to assume any sort of responsibility, so Craig took complete charge. After my transplant proved successful, I wanted to get back onto equal ground with him and be recognized as an adult. The result was a rather powerful clash of wills. As my savior and protector, Craig had unwittingly reduced my role in the relationship to that of a helpless infant. He really had no choice. My condition was so weakened, that my nerves would never have survived without Craig shielding me from the harshness of the "real" world. But it had to change, and I was determined to lessen my dependency on him, eventually reaching the point where we were again on an even footing.

It was an uphill climb. I badly needed to leave behind any trace of the sick, dependant Kelly. But Craig's now strongly engrained sense of my physical "weakness" continuously fueled his lack of confidence in my decision-making capabilities. I grew increasingly stubborn, impatient, and resentful, in spite of all the wonderful things that Craig was doing to take care of me, and us. He was *too* helpful. It drove me crazy! What he saw as caring attention, I perceived as controlling. He would write down my symptoms in my health care organizer instead of letting me do it, or correct me in front of people if I misstated even the most inconsequential fact. His admirable intention was simply to make my life as comfortable and smooth-running as possible, but his obsession with the details of my health and well-being became suffocating. Every time I made a mistake, and I made *plenty*, his instinctive response to stay in control was reinforced. Unintentionally, he was crushing any shred of self-esteem I could muster. It wasn't until I had a few climbing successes under my belt that he was willing or able to recognize my renewed strength. Then, at long last, our relationship's healthy balance was restored. Ironically, it took a mountain to get our relationship back on level ground.

Strangely enough, after my illness Craig became more of an introvert. That unflaggingly upbeat personality of his simply disappeared, surfacing only on those infrequent occasions when we got together with old pals. Our friends had their responsibilities, mostly involving kids. Although they were sympathetic and compassionate toward what we were going through, our life had become much different from theirs and we gradually grew apart, further isolating us. The man I'd married, who lived for fun and games and was never happier than when planning a backpacking getaway or other spur-of-the-moment adventure, had turned inward, and now focused much of his attention on creating space between himself and the world. Sitting at home in front of his computer became his safety zone. He stopped taking care of his emotional and physical health, and focused solely on my medical issues and on keeping us afloat financially without asking others for help. He was uncomfortable leaving me alone or under anyone else's supervision, trusting only himself to provide the level of care he felt I needed. But he never complained, seemingly resolved to his new role.

As a result of endless months of managing the early years of my illness, his career as a commercial real estate agent suffered. He lost the necessary motivation to call on prospective new customers. The effort seemed futile, since each transaction required detailed supervision for as long as a year or more. Since he didn't know what the next day might bring in terms of my health, let alone the next year, he was hesitant to become entangled in lengthy real estate transactions. As a result, he simply lost his desire to feed the sales "pipeline," and stuck mostly to referring deals to other agents. At the end of 1996, his final year in the industry, we barely eked out a living, mostly relying on our dwindling savings and my nominal disability payment. Commercial real estate in Southern California can be enormously lucrative. Craig had, like many of his colleagues, made a very handsome living. Big deals with sizable financial rewards were considered the norm. In spite of the accolades and respect he had earned from his coworkers for taking such good care of me, he was leaving at a low point, and couldn't help but feel he'd failed.

In 1997, after a three-month job search, Craig went to work as a sales rep for a local boutique shipping company. It was a very young organization, a mere four years old. Its annuity-based compensation program, coupled with a potential equity ownership opportunity, captured his interest. As well, his sales territory would be, as it had when he was in real estate, in close proximity to our house. His initial salary was small, but he viewed the "ownership" carrot as our hope for the future, and a reward suited to his value and experience. He knew if he stuck with the company that his compensation package would ultimately provide us with a comfortable living. More important, the job provided him considerable flexibility. So, if I got sick again, his solid base of clients would ensure an ongoing cash flow that would keep us afloat. This new annuity-based opportunity would be far more stable than the volatile transaction-dependent real estate business.

To make matters even more difficult for Craig, I was not happy with him taking the new sales job. I figured he had too much potential to settle for what I perceived as a glorified "delivery man." Relating his new position to the college job he held in Lake Tahoe as a driver, I couldn't help but think that his career was taking a big step backward. Craig was, after all, one of the most charismatic people I'd ever met—wonderfully creative, hugely talented, and a risk taker. From the very beginning, I'd seen "success" written all over his face. His solid performance as a commercial real estate agent during my healthy years had proven me right, and he looked the very picture of prosperity in his elegant suits and ties. Now, seeing him sporting a short-sleeve shirt emblazoned with a company logo made me cringe inside.

Though I never verbalized my disappointment, Craig could tell I thought he was selling himself short. He confronted me several times over what he sensed was my lack of support, which I always denied. As sadly superficial as it sounds, I was bothered by what our friends would think of this polished, well-educated man's unimpressive career move. Illness aside, my expectations remained high. We'd both been driven by the belief that hard work and reward go hand-in-hand, and I was disappointed by the diminished opportunity his new job seemed to offer. Deep down, I suppose I felt responsible for having derailed his life, which I subconsciously took out on him by hinting that he could do better. Also, as my health steadily improved, my "just live" philosophy was being edged out by my natural competitiveness. Shallow as it may sound, money was important to me. Although I was not seduced by material possessions, I wanted a comfortable lifestyle similar to that of my peers. It made me sick to know I could be so materialistic, but having had a transplant didn't automatically make me scuttle my ambitions. We were in our prime earning years, and I figured we needed to make hay while the sun was still shining.

Craig has never been a slave to the almighty dollar, content as long as he has the means, flexibility, and freedom to fund our adventures. He'd just as soon watch a sunset from under a tent flap than from the balcony of a five-star hotel. Though endlessly generous, Craig tends, when it comes to finances, to err on the conservative side. He saw this new job as a source of stability in our lives, something we—and, more specifically, *he*—sorely needed. Still, given his competitiveness and his innate perfectionism, I think he was ultimately hoping to be a financial success, either through ownership in the new company or in some other way. I think it was only natural to feel pressure when many of his colleagues were doing so well financially while we were in a constant state of rebuilding.

Soon, Craig *was* doing extremely well in his new position. He was steadily increasing sales, while coming up with all sorts of creative ideas to improve overall quality and efficiency. Unfortunately, about a year into the new job, he learned the owners had decided they didn't want any additional equity partners. Given how significant his contributions had been, their decision left him very disillusioned, prompting him to dust off his resume and start looking for other opportunities. Around the same time, Craig and I came up with a concept for a device that would help us monitor our hydration while exercising. We'd both experienced scary dehydration situations. In 1999, we began the process and later secured a patent for our new invention, the HydraCoach. Suddenly, the old Craig—zestful, fully motivated, and overflowing with clever ideas—was back. And, despite the scariness of embarking on a new, unproven business venture, I found myself equally charged with entrepreneurial spirit. Also, I was delighted that this bold initiative dovetailed so perfectly with our shared passion for improved health and fitness. It took years, but our homegrown concept was eventually realized in 2006, after we licensed our technology to a company that was well established in the industry.

With regard to my renewed health, I was enjoying a welcome period of sustained stability. Still, we knew it was always best to expect the unexpected. I continued my routine checkups, and during one of them, while listening to my heart with a stethoscope, Dr. Jon became aware of a significant leak in my aorta. It took me by complete surprise. So much for expecting the unexpected! In an effort to allay my fear, he told me that it's a common occurrence for most people and pretty much a sure thing among heart transplant patients. As long as it didn't compromise my lifestyle or long-term health, I reluctantly accepted his explanation. What else could I do? I was told to keep tabs on my blood pressure, because the higher the pressure, the more I'd leak. The greater the leak, the more symptomatic I would become, experiencing shortness of breath as well as all the fuss that goes along with a compromised cardiac output.

Several months later, an incident occurred that convinced me the leak was getting worse. As I sat still at night, a high-pitched, barely audible squealing noise would emanate from somewhere inside my body. It sounded like air being forced out of a leaky balloon. I was certain the leak was becoming so pronounced that I could hear it. The crazy thing is, it only happened sporadically. When I told the doctor what I was hearing, he dismissed my theory, insisting the naked ear couldn't hear a leak. From the look on his face, I got the feeling I might need to dust off that psychiatrist's card again.

Weeks ticked by, and I continued to record every time I heard it, in hope of identifying a pattern. Craig heard it too, and thought it was occurring approximately every hour. Yet, we could only hear it when I was sitting still or lying in bed. Finally, the mystery was solved. One night, I got up to go to the bathroom and Craig burst out laughing. "I know what is causing the leaky sound from your heart," he said with a broad smile. He held up my watch, which I only took off at night, always placing it on my bed stand. "Your battery is low." We were not entirely clueless; it was merely a manifestation of our underlying fear about what might happen next.

It had been four years since my transplant, and our life was finally coming together. Though fear about my illness continued to dissipate, there was one emotional element I continued to struggle with. When I was sick, I conditioned myself not to look too far into the future for fear of what might—or might *not*—be on the horizon. I visualized gazing into a crystal ball and seeing nothing. A week, or even a month, ahead I could handle, but looking further down the road was unnerving. It is a problem that still persists. I continue to get stronger and feel healthier, but remain fearful that my past might catch up with me and engulf my future. At times I find these thoughts so frightening that I personalize news of someone else getting sick. Such dispiriting notions will sneak up on me, catching me completely off guard, and put me into an emotional tailspin. I think about the impact of all the drugs I've taken and the possible damage they'll cause over time. My fretful mind keeps these worries spinning and spinning. Then, when my fears finally subside, I start to stew over the negative effects of all the extra stress. It's a vicious cycle.

Mountains remain my greatest salvation from fear and stress. I'm often asked the question, "Why do you climb?" George Leigh Mallory uttered the classic response in 1923. When asked, "Why do you want to climb Everest?" he said, "Because it's there."

My stock response may seem equally simplistic until you consider what I've been through. I climb because I can! Looking back to when I couldn't get up the stairs in my house to go to bed, it's amazing that I even talk about climbing, let alone actually do it. It's good for me physically and it's essential for me emotionally. Mountains take me into a different headspace. When consumed with everyday activities, I tend to look at life as a whole. But the very act of climbing enables me to break things into more tangible pieces. I tap into a higher awareness that allows me to simplify whatever is before me. Being on a mountain is about breathing, eating, sleeping, and moving upward toward a goal. It fills me with a blissful sense of clarity. I always return with new insight and fresh inspiration.

In my constant striving for normalcy, I avoid wearing my heart transplant on my sleeve. It would be emotional suicide. But it becomes tricky, because I have a condition that does require specific precautions, which if ignored, would compromise my health. Cleanliness, diet restrictions, reduced sun exposure (to minimize the risk of skin cancer), and medications are part of my daily lifestyle. My condition complicates even the simplest things, like having people over to the house. Try gracefully asking an adult to "please wash your hands." I dread it just as much when we are invited to be a guest in someone else's home. I sympathized with author Michael Pollan when, in his book *The Omnivore's Dilemma*, he made reference to the social awkwardness of being a vegetarian. My restrictions are much the same, and in making my dietary limitations known to the cook, it sets the tone for an awkward host–guest relationship. If I don't say anything, chances are I won't be able to eat what's being served, making the host feel bad, or insulted, or both. But if I do mention it, the cook then goes out of his or her way to make something special. It's uncomfortable any way you look at it. Bottom line: it's much easier to be finicky in a restaurant.

At other times, such as in a friendly situation where I am introduced to someone aware of my condition, the conversation inevitably turns to clichés about treasuring every waking moment, stopping to smell the flowers and living each minute as if it were your last. Invariably, my new acquaintance finds a polite way of asking, "What do the doctors say about your life expectancy?" I'm never offended; figuring it's a reasonable question, and quote the statistical average that, at the time of my transplant, I had heard was ten years. The person who posed the question typically grows quiet, and I can see them silently doing the math. Then, realizing they've just sealed my fate, they feel compelled to add something, anything. So comes the standard follow-up, "Well, you can't possibly think you are *average* in any sense of the word. Just look at everything you've done, climbing mountains and all." It's understandable. I'm the first to indulge in rationalization, telling myself that my circumstances are anything but typical. But, in one way or another everyone else does the same. It's a pretty basic coping mechanism. Eventually, though, reality swoops in. I imagine it's like being elderly. No matter how old you get, there's no way of knowing precisely how much longer you've got. But when your peers are dropping left, right, and center, you sort of figure your number will be up soon. It's the same for transplant patients. The clock starts ticking faster and faster, stealing precious moments, hours, days, and weeks. You start feeling like you're living in dog years, which reinforces the need to live now.

The other question I get all the time relates to my heart's previous owner. People are convinced I'll reveal some mysterious, even spiritual, connection between my donor and me. Novels have been written and movies made that feed this notion, but there is no scientific proof that transplanted organs have any "memory." The more logical explanation is that a transplant is a profound experience and the human mind is very susceptible to the power of suggestion. For me, the "connection" to my donor heart is that I know I have bigger shoes to fill than just my own.

I am fully aware that life can change in an instant. I learned that the moment I was diagnosed. The best way

I've found to avoid the trap of constant worry is to live purposefully. Each day I try to ensure that the rich, memorable moments outweigh the mundane ones. I love Craig's daily question, "What is the best part of your day?" I usually struggle to find the "best," so he is encouraged to ask again, and again. I'm having fun, and I live with intent. That's not the same as living each moment to the fullest. It's not that simple. I can be miserable and make everyone around me feel the same. I despise dull, repetitive, time-consuming duties like laundry or dealing with insurance claims, or having to be somewhere I don't want to be. My solution? I preplan each day, enabling me to get chores completed as quickly and efficiently as possible, allowing more time for play. As far as exercise goes, I treat it like an appointment, and it is a very important one.

Each day, whether in training for a climb or not, I strictly maintain my exercise regime. It's essential to both my physical and emotional vitality, as necessary as eating and sleeping. But, in 2000, after three years of diligent gym workouts, I was getting burned out lifting weights. I was working so hard, yet there were no visible results. It was maddening. Adding to my frustration, a few of the women who had become my gym partners, working alongside me and doing the precise same routine, did show results. As they pumped up, I remained nearly as rail thin as the first day I walked through the doors. To top it off, I had to listen to a constant chorus of complaints about cellulite, being overweight, or varicose veins. Most common was the discussion around breasts, either wanting an enhancement or being disappointed in the one they'd just paid for. They'd even ask me for diet tips, because they perceived me as so "magnificently trim." My patience grew thinner. I was there to gain back health and strength. They were there to look good in their skimpy shorts and workout tops. On my last day as a member of the gym, I was wearing one of the skimpy little tops myself, the ones the trainers look so great in—except mine wasn't quite so filled out. As I was washing up in the locker room, one woman stood staring at the massive scar on my chest. I couldn't bear it. I wanted to tell her it was a boob job that had gone horribly wrong, but some things are better left unsaid. I realized it was simply time for me to move on and find a more conducive atmosphere to fuel my body and spirit.

My timing for gym burnout was perfect. A new studio had opened nearby which offered yoga only. I had done yoga briefly before at the University of Oregon and thought it would be a good practice to go back to. It didn't take long to realize that this was for me. Yoga is different from weight training because it works from the inside out, my goal indeed. I was doing the opposite at the gym, working from the outside in. I enjoyed the flow of the postures and the focus on breathing, and in no time at all I not only felt stronger but noticed profound physical changes. I started to see small bulges where muscles were trying to appear. My endurance, balance, and flexibility improved with remarkable speed. After the surgery, my shoulders caved forward as I subconsciously tried to protect my heart. Slowly, I opened, becoming stronger, less guarded—chest forward and leading my body with my heart. One day in yoga practice I had a substitute teacher and before the class got going, she asked the students, "Does anyone have an injury?" Every single person raised his or her hand, except me. It was then that I came to the realization we all have injuries and scars of some kind. I wanted to look at my own differently. I now saw my chest scar not as a weakness or sign of trauma, but as a place where there had been an opening for change.

CHAPTER 11

A Milestone

BECAUSE the first heart transplant was performed in Africa, it seemed only appropriate to recognize that milestone medical achievement in our own special way. So, for our next challenge, Craig and I decided to conquer the Dark Continent's highest crest, Mt. Kilimanjaro. My true goal was to celebrate the many technological breakthroughs that had occurred since 1967, when Dr. Christiaan Barnard took a giant leap of faith and transplanted a heart into Mr. Louis Washkansky. Although Mr. Washkansky only survived for eighteen days, his courageous participation, along with the benevolence of his donor, Ms. Denise Darvall, paved the way for successful heart transplants all around the globe. Six years had passed since my doctors and my donor had provided me hope for a new future, and I was determined to stand on the "Roof of Africa" and serve as living proof of the progress that had been made in the field of heart transplantation.

It was autumn 2001, a paradoxical time to be organizing a celebration of life. Just as I was planning to scale one peak and shout of the life-giving goodness of transplantation and of the intense generosity demonstrated by all organ donors, two other iconic peaks were about to be toppled by terrorists whose hearts were filled with selfishness and hate.

Precisely one month after the devastating tragedy at the World Trade Center, on October 11, Craig and I were scheduled to board a plane for Tanzania. Like the rest of the world, were still in shock, mourning the senseless loss of life. Planes were initially grounded indefinitely, authorities fearful of what might happen next. The possibility of another attack on the one-month anniversary of 9/11 weighed on everyone's mind. Cautiously optimistic, we had decided we couldn't allow ourselves to be paralyzed by fear. After enduring so much, and training so hard, we did not want to be held back. If planes were flying, we agreed we'd be on our way to Africa.

Three years had passed since our 1998 sponsored "donor awareness" climb to the top of Mt. Fuji. We'd begun our search for a sponsor in mid-1999. However, due to the exorbitant cost of the expedition and the precautionary health measures associated with my travel to a Third World country, we had difficulty securing the necessary funds, and did not receive a firm commitment until fall of 2000. Our initial goal was to climb Kilimanjaro for the Millennium, but we needed the time to prepare and train. So, we decided to push back the date to October 2001.

Part of our donor awareness plan was to continue on to South Africa after our climb, meet with Dr. Barnard and visit the Groote Schuur hospital where that first heart transplant took place. (Nearly one month later, on January 6, 1968, the first U.S. transplant was successfully performed by Norman E. Shumway. Dr. Shumway developed the technique and, as such, he is known as the father of heart transplantation.) I was very much looking forward to this second stage of our African adventure.

A few weeks before our departure, my mother called with the tragic news that Dr. Barnard had suddenly died at the age of seventy-three from a severe asthma attack. I was saddened by the loss of this pioneering man whose feat had influenced countless lives. Upon hearing the news, we contacted one of Dr. Barnard's colleagues, Professor Johan Brink, who was assisting us with our visit. While a big part of our goal was to participate in a meeting that Dr. Brink had arranged with Dr. Barnard, he encouraged us to still come, meet him and the other surgeons, and continue on with our planned tribute. Looking back, I realize it was privilege enough to know that Dr. Barnard was aware of what I was about to attempt.

We still intended to go, but were encountering problems with the required immunizations to enter Cape Town. We found ourselves caught up in miles of red tape that required endless emails, letters, and telephone calls to untangle and stretched our patience to its absolute limit. The stumbling block was the yellow fever vaccination that anyone traveling to South Africa is required to have, if arriving from a country listed as infected with yellow fever. Because we'd be traveling from Tanzania (where Kilimanjaro is located) to Kenya (where yellow fever is present), we had to be vaccinated. I could get the typical Typhoid, Cholera, Tetanus, and Hepatitis vaccines. No problem. But, our tropical disease doctor informed us that the yellow fever vaccination wasn't an option for me because it is a live virus and is, due to my immunosuppression, ill-advised. In an attempt to get around the issue, Craig contacted the South African Embassy for a waiver, but was denied. The only alternative was a six-day quarantine period. But since people in quarantine are likely ill, and possibly contagious, that wasn't an option either. We looked for help anywhere we could, calling our outfitter, the doctors at Groote Schuur and the doctors' government contacts. Finally, we were told to bring a letter explaining my condition, and to have the vaccine certificate stamped and signed, indicating that the vaccination is contraindicated. I was also provided a contact name in South Africa, in case we were detained after disembarking in Johannesburg.

Traveling to Africa presents several health-related risks. In addition to yellow fever, there's the dangerous threat of malaria. To protect ourselves from the mosquito-borne disease, we had to take Larium once a week, beginning two weeks prior to departure and continuing until four weeks after we'd returned home, as a prophylactic. The side effects are severe anxiety, depression, hallucinations, and even a few reported cases of suicide. (That final worry was of no concern to me. I'd already more than proven my will to live!)

Most people who visit exotic destinations fret about more common complications, such as diarrhea. But I wasn't like most people. Because of my immunosuppression, I had to be extra cautious. We met with two specialists. Initially, we saw Dr. Panosian, an infectious disease/travel doctor at UCLA, an obvious choice as she had internal access to my medical records. After hearing our request, she tried to talk us out of going. When I first mentioned we needed shots for our East Africa trip to climb Kilimanjaro, she was absolutely fine with it—until I told her I'd had a heart transplant. In response to the surprised expression on her face, I bolstered my case by explaining my goal, and more importantly, the fact that I already had the blessing of Dr. Jon. Ignoring my every word, she launched into a lengthy dissertation on every conceivable risk that might be waiting in the African wilds. Clearly not amused, she finally said, "There are lots of scenic places in this world. Why risk your life thousands of miles from home on Kilimanjaro?" Taking her advice in stride, we went in search of a second opinion.

Seeking out a doctor who is going to tell you what you want to hear is not a practice I condone; but, in this case, I needed another professional viewpoint. I knew precisely who to seek out. I made an appointment with Dr. Wallace, another infectious disease specialist, whom I'd seen after I was first diagnosed with my heart virus back in 1992. Reflecting on our history and our character, she had faith in me, and Craig, and subsequently took it upon herself to help pave the way. She obtained special waivers and permission, lined up the appropriate contacts, and even wrote to the South African Embassy on our behalf. We were encouraged by her resourcefulness and enthusiasm.

Our goal was, literally and figuratively, enormous. Mt. Kilimanjaro proudly stands at 19,340 feet and is one of the world's Seven Summits, representing the tallest mountain on each continent, a goal of many career mountaineers. I had never hiked above 14,496 feet, the elevation of Mt. Whitney. Furthermore, this climb would be a winding, eight-day ascent covering roughly forty-five miles. When I heard we'd secured the funding, I immediately stepped up the pace and started to train rigorously. My diligence had already paid off. Just as I had intended, more powerful muscles in my back, arms, and legs helped pluck oxygen from the blood much more efficiently, which meant less stress on my heart.

My primary training ground moved from the local hills to the higher peaks surrounding the Owens Valley basin. White Mountain, standing 14,250 feet, became a frequent place Craig and I would visit, proving to be an ideal location to test a variety of high altitude remedies, as my goal was to exceed this height by more than 5,000 feet. This was revealing in and of itself, as the level of my training was nearly matching my greatest climbing accomplishment thus far. To be reminded of this, as I stood on White Mountain's summit, I could look across the valley toward Mt. Whitney. I had newfound strength and, with it, greater confidence.

Though I felt physically ready, medical tests were still required to provide Dr. Jon with the information he needed to give his blessing. He had to confirm if my strength was in my head or truly in my heart. Because of the extreme elevation I hoped to reach, we all agreed it was prudent to also perform a VO2 Max test, also known as a cardiopulmonary stress test. To measure VO2, I had to exert myself on a treadmill, working my lungs as hard as I could. When my body reached its exhaustion point and my lungs reached their maximum output, my VO2 score was established. My results indicated my heart function was 68 percent of normal, meaning "average" for a healthy, nontransplant person. I was told my results were very good and that most heart transplant patients are 40 to 50 percent. I could feel discouraged that I had worked so hard and was still only 70 percent of "average," or I could embrace the very good assessment. Naturally, since I was much stronger than I had been, I decided not to let a mere number hold me back.

Just a week before leaving, we were invited to attend a special, intimate event honoring Dr. Kawata, the senior doctor of my cardiovascular medical group. It was held at his home, and included a few of his physician colleagues as well as some key pharmaceutical company representatives, including our trip sponsor. Toward the end of the evening, we were all called together to toast the accomplishments of this devoted man. Then, our upcoming climb was "officially" announced. I had been standing in one place for some time and could feel my blood pressure falling. I thought I was going to faint. Craig stood behind me, propping me up like a puppet as, for what seemed an eternity, we waited for each person to add his or her comments. As the focus of attention slowly shifted away from me, we quickly sought out a quiet corner where I could lie down and regain my composure. Here I was, the "mighty Kelly" wilting in front of my most important supporters—and my sponsors!

Once again, we contacted our journalist friend Brendan, who put us in touch with AP's South African bureau chief. Because all three of his staff writers were subsequently busy with post–9/11 coverage, he couldn't assign anyone to our story. Instead, it was decided Brendan would report on our climb while he remained in the United States. In addition, thanks to contacts made through the California Heart Center Foundation (formerly known as Gift of the Heart Foundation), Michael Brown of Serac Adventure Films was hired to join us and document our climb. Our team was greatly comforted by the welcome news that Michael had already made two ascents up Mt. Everest, one of which included the filming of Erik Weihenmayer, the first blind man to reach the famed peak. In fact, we later learned from Michael and Erik, two consummate pranksters, that when Michael got the first request to participate in our adventure, he thought it was Erik pulling his leg. Michael wondered, first a blind man and now a heart recipient climbing one of the world's seven summits? It had to be a joke.

This was our most ambitious climb yet, and would be widely discussed within the medical community. It was going to be a monumental feat for me to get up there, and would take a fiercely dedicated team effort to pull it off. Joining us again for added security was our friend Susan, along with Michael's camera assistant Chris. Rounding out the team was Bobby from the outfitter, four African guides and forty porters, most of whom spoke only Swahili. Having local porters shoulder trekkers' belongings is standard practice on this climb, and provides them the opportunity to earn a decent income. Everyone, even the porters, was aware of my condition and delighted to be part of such an unprecedented adventure. The energy and excitement was building every day.

With so much at stake, I was being extra conscientious, careful not to court danger, get injured, or get sick. Well, accidents happen. Just three days before we were scheduled to depart, I was playing, doing a yoga handstand in my hallway at home. Suddenly, I fell back, twisting my ankle as I landed. The pain was excruciating and my ankle swelled to several times its normal size. It became so bloated that I feared I'd never be able to put on my hiking boot. Craig rushed me to the emergency room at Saddleback Hospital, and when I explained through my tears that I was planning to climb Mt. Kilimanjaro, the doctor stared at me in disbelief and announced, "You're not going to be climbing anything!" Two days later I was walking as if the injury had never happened. Miraculously, I had *willed away* the swelling. The next day, we were Africa-bound.

It was early morning at LAX, and I felt as though I'd crossed over into the Twilight Zone. Thanks to the well-publicized "high security alert," the terminal was nearly empty except for yellow police tape and extra security checkpoints. It was odd to feel so unsafe on your own turf, but I couldn't wait to get out of the L.A. area airspace. I felt a little guilty leaving at a time of such national sadness, but once I got on the plane, I stayed focused on our upcoming adventure. I had to; the flight was nineteen hours, not including a layover in Amsterdam.

We arrived in Arusha, Tanzania, and headed to a small building that more resembled a carport than an airport, and with far less security. We were met by our outfitter and taken away on a single-lane paved road until we turned off onto a dirt path through the bushes. It was creepy—no lights, no people, just dark, lush, and overgrown. After several bumpy miles, the road opened onto what looked like a rustic estate lifted straight from the movie *Out of Africa*. We drove up, and were met by three beautiful African women turned out in white dresses and black aprons. They collected our luggage and showed us to an exotically renovated barn that doubled as an elegant bar and restaurant. We walked in to find our midnight snack beautifully laid out—thinly sliced, grass-fed beef and chicken alongside a crystal decanter of red wine. I was ready to move in permanently. We went to bed knowing we would be able to luxuriate in this utopia for three days, readjusting our bodies after the long flight and shaking off any lingering jet lag before commencing our climb. We awoke the next morning to a spectacular view. In the foreground were gemlike guest cottages scattered throughout a massive garden, along with stables and an adjacent polo field. In the distance stood the tantalizing outline of Mt. Kilimanjaro.

We spent an entire day hiking nearby on the spectacular volcano of Mt. Meru, learning everything we could about the region and its wildlife. We started off traveling by Land Rover past a vibrant array of birds and animals, including bushbuck, zebra, eland, oryx and, through the trees, giraffes. The vastness and beauty of the African plains overwhelmed me. We continued on above the grasslands toward the lush forest, inhabited by wild birds and black-and-white Colobus monkeys, swinging freely from one tree limb to the next. I was surprised to discover that our guide carried a rifle. He explained that, though it is a required piece of equipment, he had no intention of using it. In fact, if he found himself in a situation where he had to shoot, he could be reprimanded or possibly even lose his job. As peaceful as the animals appeared to be, it was a reminder of the dangers of the wild, and that we were guests in their home. I was both mesmerized and energized by the day's events, the actual trekking taking a back seat to all the activity around us. And this was just the beginning.

Over the next couple of days, Craig and Susan found themselves still coping with the ill effects of the time difference. I, however, was raring to go. The arduous trek up Mt. Kilimanjaro would take us though five climate zones, from the cultivated land slopes and lush tropical rainforest to the rainy alpine Moorlands and barren highlands desert and, finally, on to the frigid winds of the Arctic zone and the glacier-capped summit. We chose the Machame or "champagne" Route, because it is the least traveled and most scenic. While most trekkers spend a total of five days on the mountain, we'd scheduled eight, allowing more time for acclimatization and increasing our chances of reaching the summit.

The first day we met up with our guides before hitting the trail. One of them, whose adopted English name was Honest, wanted us to know he was a fervent supporter of the United States. To prove his point, he wore a red, white, and blue American bandana the entire time. He and the others guides were most sympathetic about what we had just experienced in our homeland. It was amazing to see that, distant as they were from New York's concrete corridors, they too were touched, both emotionally and economically, by the devastating events of 9/11.

We made our way up the beginning of the trail. The path was beautiful, leading us through a dense forest of fig and rubber trees, begonias, and other tropical vegetation. Though the trek didn't seem too daunting, I experienced the first of many challenges. The worse thing I can do is underestimate any part of a climb, especially since my engine relies on the "fire" of adrenaline. But that's precisely what I did. I had been told time and time again that the trail was easy. One guidebook even called it "a stroll at high altitude." While that may have been a fair description, for my body the first day was terribly demanding. Overexertion at this early stage, along with the corresponding anxiety, was like a red flag waving in the African breeze. By the time I reached Machame Camp, our first stop at 9,100 feet, I tearfully expressed to Craig how frustrating the day had been, telling him, "That was *so* hard, and it didn't help that you were learning Swahili while I was simply trying to catch my breath!"

While we were carrying light loads in comfortable, supportive backpacks, the porters whizzed past us with heavy loads balanced precariously on their heads or backs. I watched as an unending supply of fresh foods—including eggs, potatoes, chicken, and even watermelon—flew by. It was humbling to see. In a less than flattering way, I felt I represented the "wimpification" of the New World. It drove home how fortunate we are and emphasized the chasm between our societies, separating the haves from the have-nots. They worked so hard, we could smell them coming as they drew close. As a tip to save our energy, they would say, "Pole, pole" in Swahili, meaning "slowly, slowly." Everyone—the guides and my teammates— seemed so strong, further magnifying how hard the day had been for me.

Our wake-up call came at 6:00 A.M. A peek outside the tent revealed that the expected rain and cold were rolling in. To help us warm up, we were greeted with steaming coffee and cocoa. After a quick breakfast, it was time to go. The day's trek took us up a steep track through a savannah of tall grasses, volcanic rock, and bearded heather. By the time we got to Shira Camp (altitude: 11,300 feet), we were soaked, but the hardworking porters had arrived well ahead of us and had everything set up. As part of the acclimatizing process, this would be our home for the next two nights. I loved the rich earth tone background of the surrounding landscape against the vibrant yellow igloo-style tents. They seemed to brightly convey the spirit of our adventure. In stark contrast to these playful, lemon-colored dots, stood a large, imposing green tent, where the entire group shared meals, games, and conversation, and where all our planning took place.

I did great the second day, but the third was difficult. We woke to a thin, pristine layer of snow and ice covering the ground and our tents. The frigid wind numbed my face. Two hours into our acclimatization hike, while making our way to 13,000 feet, I began to get the all too familiar feeling of nausea that signaled low blood pressure, causing me to collapse. Just like that, I hit the ground. Craig jumped into action, elevating my feet to restore the blood flow to my head and quickly placing the blood pressure cuff around my arm. It was unexpected and alarming, a harsh reminder to everyone of my precarious condition. Given my state, we decided to call it a day and make our way down to Shira Camp. While everyone was admiring the sunset blaze of orange, yellow, and pink surrounding distant Mt. Meru, I lay in my tent, trying to settle my churning stomach. Later, as my nausea worsened, I began dry heaving. It was time to reevaluate the order and dose of my drugs. Dicey as it was to alter my medication schedule, I knew, given my current condition, that there was little chance of me making it through the next day, let alone to the summit, if I didn't do something. This was especially true in a Third World country like Africa, and remote at that! The next morning, nausea gone and energy renewed, I knew I'd made the right decision.

This was the first time I'd ever participated in a film project. The first few days I didn't really pay much attention. I was more focused on my health. Thankfully, Michael was as unobtrusive as he could be. Initially I expected him to be close to me, sticking the camera in my face. He was just the opposite. I didn't see him much at all. His demeanor delighted me. He was the ultimate outdoorsman—tall, strong as an ox, and fast as he carried his heavy cameras and equipment, dashing up ahead or scurrying to the side of us to get the perfect shot. His natural affinity to high altitudes was obvious. While he leapt around like a mountain goat, I felt lucky just to be able to catch my breath and walk straight.

By day four, we could sense the gain in elevation, as a thick layer of clouds blanketed the valley below us. I was growing increasingly aware that this was an adventure different from any other. Our steady walk took us up to the pass at Lava Tower (15,000 feet), surpassing my or any other heart transplant's altitude record. Setting a new benchmark was, excuse the pun, a new high for me. I was absolutely exhilarated. My heart was strong and I felt great. After we shared a high-five and took a moment to savour our accomplishment, we began our descent, again part of the acclimatization process, to Barranco Camp.

Over the next two days, we logged close to twenty hours of hiking, crossing the Karanga Valley, where giant Lobelia grow, then making our way to Camp Barafu, perched at 15,500 feet on the northern slope of the crater. This would be our base camp for summit day.

We arrived early and quickly went to bed, knowing that, in traditional alpine style, we would begin our bid for the summit at midnight. I followed my usual routine as I prepared for bed, checking my blood pressure, oxygen saturation, and heart rate. I could hear the guides getting out the hyperbaric chamber, which, in case of emergency, simulates a lower altitude. They were testing it to make sure it was in working order before we moved skyward. As cozy and tired as we were, we tossed and turned, sleepless with excitement, knowing all our years of planning and hard work would come down to the next twenty-four hours. Contributing to our sleeplessness was the growing wind that began to batter our tent. At first, we thought it was going to subside, but as the night grew on, it grew in intensity. At the stroke of midnight, we made our way to the common tent to meet our climbing partners. They were also concerned over the increasing wind. But having made it this far, we decided as a group to stick with our plans, and headed into the black abyss. I was relatively comfortable in the beginning, fueled by adrenaline but wary of the imposing zero degree temperature, not including wind chill. Forget that the oxygen is about half of that at sea level, that surface water is practically nonexistent and that, at these dizzy heights, only a few hardy spiders can survive; the perishing cold was far too inhospitable for just about any life form.

The fifty-mile-an-hour wind gusts were torturous, nipping away at my physical and emotional energy. Periodically, the entire team would surround and shield me from the full impact of the blasts. I weighed barely one-hundred pounds, and the frigid wind easily penetrated all my layers of clothing. Impossible as it was to conceal how cold I was, I certainly didn't want to let on that I might need help. I felt no body heat, as if my blood had frozen in my veins. Desperation set in as I tried to figure out what I could do to build up energy and heat. At one point, while we all huddled together, Michael said, "You're going to need extra protection! Let me give you my stuff." He took off his heavy down jacket, which fit me like a puffy dress, and bundled me inside it, and then had me put on his thick gloves. He had generated so much body warmth that the jacket and gloves felt heated. Michael put on his spare jacket and used my smaller down jacket as makeshift gloves. I was so grateful to him, knowing what an enormous sacrifice he was making on my behalf, and knew the best way to demonstrate my gratitude was to simply keep going. Meanwhile, trailing us a short distance behind was a group of Australians, who made a different choice and turned back. It was disquieting seeing their stream of headlights retreating in unison away from the coveted prize that they likely had trained so hard to conquer. I reached into my reserves and walked slowly, struggling to avoid being blown over by the wind. A few times I desperately wanted to rest, but was afraid to stop, knowing my heart delay would result in more work than continuing at a slow pace. I started to do the "rest step," resting on one leg then bringing the rear foot up even with the forward foot, rather than stepping past it. It is a well-known method of conserving energy, and I needed to conserve every ounce I could! Realizing there were still a couple more hours before daylight, I prayed for that first glimmer of light, knowing that if I could stick it out until then, the sun would rise and the winds would begin to taper off.

But the winds were still so fierce that I had to keep my head down. Craig repositioned himself in front of me to set the pace and to block the full force of the gusts. Everyone was focused on my welfare. In one of our final huddles, Chris turned to me and said, "You know, you need to do this on your own!" I was totally insulted, silently smoldering and thinking, "why would you think I wouldn't want to do this on my own?" Then, I realized I'd simply misinterpreted his intention. He was not being mean-spirited, but was trying to motivate me. He wanted me to find the strength within myself to make it happen; it was up to me to reveal what I had.

We reached the volcanic rim of the mountain, just 340 vertical feet from the highest point, and stopped to celebrate this significant milestone. I turned around to give Craig a hug and, to my surprise, found him flat on his back and without his top insulating layers. It was like déjà vu, seeing him sprawled on the ground. Once again, he had hit the altitude wall, and hard! He had spent the last few hours acting as my human windshield, as well as giving me his food and water, as my supply had become buried somewhere deep within my layers. At this point it was too dangerous for him to proceed. As much as he wanted to push himself, he didn't want to risk having to use the emergency equipment and then not have it available for me.

Quietly, Craig said to me, "Kelly, our goal for this climb was never about me making it to the top. It was always bigger than that. It's to get you safely up and safely down this mountain. That's what matters."

I remained completely bundled up to protect myself from the cold, while Craig continued to strip down as though he had just arrived at a hot, sunny beach. The frozen sun was glinting off Craig's sunglasses while he described his all too familiar symptoms. As he prepared to head down to base camp, I could tell by the way his body was wavering how unstable and sick he felt. He assured me he could make it down the mountain, and that I shouldn't worry. I hugged him, wanting him to know what I couldn't put into words. I wanted to give him strength, just as he had helped me be strong so many times over the years. Most of all, I wanted him to know how moved I was that, even when feeling so terribly ill, he thought of my safety and comfort first. I knew how much he had wanted to reach the top of the mountain with me. My heart broke. As he waved goodbye to me, I knew deep down it was Craig who had the true courage.

I was more determined than ever to make Craig proud of me. When I reached the summit, I felt such exhilaration. I knew that Craig would want me to savor and celebrate the moment and, even though he wasn't physically near me, I felt him by my side, cheering for me. The sky was a magnificent blue and a tall glacier was gleaming in the sunlight as I stood on the mountain's crest. There is a sign at the peak of Kilimanjaro that says, "The Roof of Africa." When I first saw it, the headiness of the milestone was crystallized. I felt particularly moved because I was standing at the highest point on the continent that was home to Dr. Barnard. I carried with me a tribute letter, cowritten with one Dr. Barnard's South African colleagues. It included his favorite poem, "A Bag of Tools," written by R. L. Sharpe. After glancing at it one last time, I left it in the metal box at the summit.

> Each is given a bag of tools,
> A shapeless mass,
> A book of rules;
> And each must make—
> Ere life is flown—
> A stumbling block
> Or a stepping-stone.

I had made it to one of the world's "seven summits." In a profound way, I felt Craig and I had come full circle. Before my transplant, when we were first climbing Mt. Whitney, Craig had had to turn around before making it to the top. Now, it was as if we were as we had been, before I had had any problems with my heart. Once again, Craig had to turn back. Once again, I was strong enough to reach the top on my own. But we were still a team: he was with me on this mountaintop. I could feel it. We had made this climb together. His strength, courage, and love were in my heart.

Thrilled as I was, I was more anxious to get back and see Craig, make sure he was okay, and tell him the good news. As I approached base camp, fifteen hours after the start of the climbing day, I saw him coming up to greet me. I was so happy he was standing! He greeted me with a big hug, teary congratulations and, of course, a little felt bag with my charm. Using my swollen, sausagelike fingers, I carefully opened the bag. It was incredible, again a perfect replica of the distinctly shaped mountain, and the fourth charm on my growing bracelet.

That night, now acclimatized to the elevation, we all slept well. After a long trek down the next day, the expedition ended with the entire forty-plus person support team gathering around to sing their traditional celebratory song. With grinning faces and hands clapping in unison, it was apparent they knew this adventure was more significant than most. After all, they were part of the team that got the first heart transplant recipient to the top of their famous mountain.

The next day we were off to Kenya, then to South Africa to visit the Groote Schuur Hospital. As exhausted as I was, I was still on top of the mountain, full of energy and ready for an adventure. We made our way to Cape

Town, the Mother City of Africa. It is one of the most beautiful regions in the world and a rich cultural melting pot, due to the amalgamation of Indonesian, French, Dutch, British, and German settlers. As planned, we met with Dr. Brink and his colleagues, and were taken to the OR where that historic first transplant was performed. It had been painstakingly restored and equipped to resemble its original state. Even the hospital gowns were original (though, frankly, very little has changed about these frumpy garments, which seem to have gotten locked in a universal time capsule!) In an adjacent room, were all sorts of fascinating memorabilia, including photographs, documents, equipment, instruments, and other artifacts related to that seismic medical breakthrough.

In one article, I came upon a profound quote, made by Dr. Barnard in reference to those brave heart patients who agreed to participate in those first, risky transplants: "For a dying man it is not a difficult decision, because he knows he is at the end. If a lion chases you to the bank of a river filled with crocodiles, you will leap into the water convinced you have a chance to swim to the other side. But you would never accept such odds if there were no lion."

How true is that. In looking around, it was clear that time was on my side. The equipment was not only antiquated, but looked big, bulky, noisy and, worst of all, painful! How much I appreciate having my health problems now vs. then. In the same spirit, I hope future patients make similar remarks about today's technology.

One of the most interesting people I learned and read about was Hamilton Naki. He assisted Dr. Barnard with the first transplant in 1967 and later became part of his regular team. However, the first transplant happened during the height of apartheid, and because he was black, his contribution was kept secret for nearly thirty years. He was initially hired to be a hospital gardener and later asked to help with the laboratory animals. He quickly progressed from cleaning cages, working his way up to becoming Dr. Barnard's right-hand man. According to the professor, "Hamilton Naki had better technical skills than I did," he said. "He was a better craftsman than me, especially when it came to stitching, and had very good hands." Tragically, despite his skills, the political climate of the day barred any recognition of his work. Instead, Naki was prohibited both from studying to be a doctor and from the *whites-only* operating theater. So, though he stood by Dr. Barnard's side, his accomplishments as one of a pioneering surgeon's leading assistants was lost in the dark shadow of the time. Deep inside, he had to feel as though the patient was not the only one with a knife in his heart. Fortunately, his valuable contributions have since been made well known, wonderful proof that progress has been made not only medically but also socially.

After meeting and touring the facility, we were honored with an invitation to meet a few local heart transplant recipients as well as Dr. Barnard's daughter, Deirdre and her husband Kobus, at the top of Table Mountain. To illustrate that heart transplant patients can resume active lives, I was again put to the test. There is a cable car to the top. Instead of riding comfortably, I was asked to join Dr. Brink and a group of local heart recipients in a hike to our destination. I was thrilled, but exhausted. Table Mountain stands a mere 3,500 feet, nothing compared to the summit I'd reached just days before. But after so grueling an eight-day climb, a speed bump looked imposing to me. It was a steep and tough hike, my muscles were sore and stiff, and my body fussed all the way up. But just as I have done in the past, I proceeded slowly, gently placing one foot in front of the other. It was worth every labored breath. At the top, there is a small café and wraparound deck offering spectacular views in all directions. I met Deirdre and we briefly got acquainted. She told me that her dad would have been honored by my visit and tribute. But the pleasure was mine. My success was his success! As we said our good-byes, I gave her a copy of the tribute and poem, identical to the ones I'd placed at the top of Mt. Kilimanjaro and donated to the Groote Schuur museum.

Later that evening, we looked back toward Table Mountain, Cape Town's most famous landmark. As the night air cooled, clouds began to flow over the edge like a breaking wave, what is appropriately called the "table-cloth." Legend has it that Van Hunks, an old Afrikaner, retired from sailing the seven seas, would often go to his favorite spot on top of the Mountain to smoke his pipe. One day, a stranger showed up. When Van Hunks boasted about how much he could smoke, this man replied that he could smoke just as much. This angered Van Hunks, and he challenged the stranger to a smoking competition. The stranger turned out to be the devil. The reason the tablecloth appears? Because they both just keep puffing away and neither ever wins! I felt I was right there, part of a legend, or in my case—fairy tale.

We arrived home on November 5. As expected, we were exhausted from jet lag and all the excitement of traveling to the other side of the world. That same day, Craig noticed a mysterious red mark on his ankle that appeared to be a bite. Just a day later, he began to feel flu-like symptoms, including fever and swollen glands. Later in the week, Craig went to see a doctor at the local Urgent Care who looked him over and said, "It's nothing." But Craig's intuition told him otherwise. So, he drove to Pasadena to see Dr. Wallace, our infectious disease doctor, and was immediately sent to the emergency room and subsequently admitted. She had no definite diagnosis, but figured it was best to treat it as though it was an insect-borne disease. Not knowing the specific source of his symptoms, it was required that he be quarantined and wait for proper diagnosis. Due to my own condition, I couldn't visit him in the isolated area. Not only was this scary for both of us, but I felt tremendous guilt about not being able to be with him after he had spent virtually every night in the hospital with me. After three days of blood tests and IV antibiotics, his fever broke and he was sent home with an additional six weeks worth of medication. A few weeks later, his diagnosis was determined: tick-borne Typhus Fever. This is a disease similar to Rocky Mountain spotted fever. As careful as we were, using repellants, covering all exposed skin with clothing and prompt removal of any attached ticks, we were surprised to have this happen. Thank God it wasn't some Ebola type-disease, and how fortunate that his symptoms didn't surface until we were back in California. I hate to imagine us embarking on a search for a sterile clinic in the wilds of Africa.

It's amazing. I am the sick person here, yet it seems Craig ends up with his own complications every time we leave the country. Just after returning from Japan to climb Mt. Fuji, he had contracted chicken pox. Now, he'd come home with an African tick. It was as if Craig was my medical shield, attracting all the bugs (literally and figuratively!) that my weakened immune system couldn't have handled.

Several months after the trip, I was contacted by a London-based company that was organizing a media event for a project called Kili-Liver-Live. Dr. Jacques

Pirenne, a Belgian doctor who specializes in liver transplants, was leading it. He was also a mountain climber, and planned to take a group of six liver recipients to Africa and attempt to summit Kilimanjaro. To help raise awareness of the trip and reinforce the message that there is active life after a transplant, Craig and I were invited to share our Kilimanjaro experience at a media briefing. While they would not face the challenges of denervation, what I have in common with liver transplant patients is drugs, many of which are the same. Also, I could provide a first-hand account of the altitude-related issues we faced, particularly as they pertained to drug and food metabolism and the associated side effects. We hoped my experience would prove helpful as they began training for their exciting adventure.

What made the event even more exciting was that it was being held in Monte Carlo. After the press conference and plenty of lively discussion with the enthusiastic Kili-Liver-Live team, we met up with a photographer and TV reporter who interviewed us in our hotel room, then shot supplementary footage of us walking the waterfront in front of the Garibaldi Forum.

Craig recalled our previous visit to Monte Carlo, during our anniversary trip in 1992, just before I got sick. The train conductor had confiscated our passports because our tickets weren't properly activated. He made no attempt to speak English or help us understand what was going on. So, when he departed, we figured we were headed to jail. Craig's recollection got me thinking. What if, those nine long years ago, we'd been able to peer into the future and, standing in almost the same spot in the middle of Monte Carlo, seen ourselves strolling near the water's edge with a camera crew trailing behind us. What, we surely would have wondered, had happened in our lives to enable us to attract our own, private paparazzi?

Five of the six Belgian patients not only reached the summit, but also adopted our tradition and blew bubbles in celebration! When they returned, we received a signed t-shirt from the team as well as a slew of emails. Frank, one of the trekkers wrote, "Kelly, you were our security, [proving the] project was feasible. Thank you. I will always remember your dynamism in Monaco, giving us hope for doing it!"

Interestingly, two years later, Dr. Panosian, the infectious disease specialist who initially discouraged us from going to Africa, wrote an article about our meeting in the *L.A. Times*. She said she wanted to retract her advice. Fearful of my health, she admitted she'd been silently envisioning dusty clinics with broken X-Ray machines, pharmacies in broom closets, etc. She was worried what would happen should I need serious medical help. Then she said, "The same moment I told them they should travel somewhere else, I regretted it and, in voicing my fear, I forgot Kelly's courage."

CHAPTER 12

The Climb of
My Life

IT was 2003, and my "new" heart was approaching its eighth birthday. That "ten-year average life expectancy" statistic weighed heavily on my mind. I didn't feel I had the luxury to wait before ticking another destination off my "dream" list. Craig and I decided it was time to set our sights on the Matterhorn. Given the roles both the original and its Disneyland replica played at the onset of my illness, I figured it would be particularly triumphant to conquer that majestic peak anew. Nor did it hurt that the Matterhorn was, and remains, one of the most recognized and revered mountains in the world, a fact that would help us further bring attention to the worldwide need for organ donation.

Actually, it was impossible for us to escape that grand Alpine peak. A quaint curio, brought back from Switzerland by Craig when he first visited in 1978 had hung in our hallway ever since we were married. It features a miniature Matterhorn, complete with a grey-haired climber carrying a rucksack and ice axe while dangling from a thin string. When you pull on the rope, it plays the tune "Edelweiss," as the little guy rocks his way up the mountainside. Every time I passed it, I couldn't resist pulling the string and finding myself soothed by the sweet lullaby that Christopher Plummer made world famous in *The Sound of Music.*

In preparation for this climb, which would be our toughest and most technically challenging yet, we trained in ways we never had before. We were successful in securing the necessary financial backing through our supporters at the California Heart Center Foundation who were equally enthusiastic about our landmark quest. Joining us on the climb would be Michael, our cinematographer friend who accompanied us on Kilimanjaro, as well as our mountain guide Jean, and his apprentice Tim. Jean was chosen because, at that time, he had climbed the Matterhorn more than seventy times, an accomplishment matched by few. The Matterhorn was going to be a real endurance test, demanding rock-climbing agility, the ability to acclimate to the nearly 15,000-foot peak, and requiring a concerted team effort.

With our climb quickly approaching, we immediately began our altered style of training. In addition to frequent outdoor trips to Tahquitz, Joshua Tree, and Yosemite California, we joined a local rock-climbing gym and spent most evenings and weekends finessing our way up challenging routes, both of us becoming reasonably skilled at sport climbing. Our Matterhorn ascent would require greater focus on the technical side of mountaineering, adding to the freshness and appeal of the challenge. In no time at all, we became more proficient than ever at climbing techniques, equipment, knots, and rappelling.

After an intensely concentrated program of training, conditioning, and planning, we were ready to go. When we first arrived in the small village of Zermatt, Switzerland, in August 2003, clouds shrouded the Matterhorn, making it look like the star performer waiting for the curtain to rise on opening night. The next day, as we were walking through town, the clouds dissipated, revealing the pyramid-shaped peak. My first reaction was, "My God! What were we thinking?" At that moment, I felt like an entire flock of butterflies was winging through my stomach. The treacherous slopes and precipitous, narrow ridges looked intimidating and unforgiving. It was easy to see why the Matterhorn's steep paths had proved fatal to more than five hundred climbers. To add to my own growing trepidation, the summer had been unseasonably hot, resulting in far more melting ice and permafrost than normal, causing dangerous conditions. There had been closures throughout the Alps, including the Matterhorn where, just three weeks earlier, an unprecedented seventy people had to be evacuated by helicopter when a major rock tower collapsed, blocking the primary route. Our timing could not have been worse.

A day later, Michael arrived from Colorado, and together we met Jean and Tim. Tim would be there to assist Michael with his camera equipment and would participate in our training climbs. Because it was determined that the most efficient way to achieve a successful summit would be via a one-to-one guide-to-climber ratio, Jean arranged to have one more mountain guide, Cedric, join us later in the trip. He would serve as Craig's guide on the day of the final ascent.

Jean is an interesting guy. During our initial meeting he was very charismatic and fun loving, but didn't hold back about how utterly serious he was about the climb. While I am the first to take mountains seriously, I have always enjoyed being driven by the intense passion of other climbers. The minute Jean put on his guide helmet, his affable nature turned authoritative and commanding, which caused an issue later in our adventure. He explained to us that speed was imperative to a successful Alpine summit. Speed is, of course, my Achilles' heel because of my quirky cardiac output. But, I figured all I could do was my best.

The next few days were built around training climbs, allowing Jean to get acquainted with our skill levels, thresholds, pacing, personalities (particularly, how each of us handled stress) and overall endurance. What better place, we figured, than the Alps—the birthplace of mountain climbing—to hone our skills. Where on some previous climbs we'd been able to get away with just a good pair of boots and some hiking poles, now we were laden with ropes, harnesses, crampons, and ice axes. I approached each new piece of equipment with a sense of curiosity, eager to learn everything I could. It was all tremendous fun, until we had to carry all the extra weight. The porters on Kilimanjaro had spoiled us, and it wasn't long before I was thinking how nice it would be to have Honest along to ease my burden.

The first day of training we loaded our backpacks and made our way to the small Alpine town of Saas Fe, nestled in a valley next to Zermatt. We hiked a steep ascent from the valley floor to the Almageller Mountain Hütte, our home for the following three nights. The hut system adds a layer of rustic luxury to the beauty of climbing in Europe. I hesitate in using the term "hut" as it doesn't begin to convey the superb accommodations we were afforded. The hütte was more like a bed and breakfast—family owned, very clean, with a restaurant-style dining room offering fresh, homemade cuisine and, naturally, beer and wine. Even more satisfying than the delectable local treats was the tremendous camaraderie with interesting people from all over the world.

Jean's scrupulousness extended to careful supervision of my dietary restrictions. He knew that I avoided fatty foods, including anything fried or with cream, cheese, or butter sauce. It wasn't easy. Swiss food is an amalgamation of German, Italian, and French cuisine, all known for heavy sauces and sausages. Peering over the menu, we determined that about 90 percent of it was verboten for me. Jean talked to the manager of the hut and informed her of my limitations, but it was too late; she had already planned her meals for the upcoming week and had by then received all her supplies by helicopter. Jean knew he needed to do something. So, unbeknownst to me, he consulted with Craig before the climb and snuck away to a local market to pick up a package of lean turkey filets. I didn't really think about food after our initial conversation, as I always bring along an emergency ration of prepackaged tuna, just in case. Still, I prefer to blend in as best I can and eat what I can of whatever is being served. As dinnertime approached, I remained optimistic that the cook would have something I could eat. Upon concluding that, among the available options, I'd be limited to boiled potatoes and plain pasta, Craig told me of Jean's shopping expedition. I was delighted by his generosity. Experience has taught me that carbohydrates alone, in combination with my primary medications, will throw my stomach into a tailspin at high altitudes. The best antidote, outside of antinausea drugs, is plain lean protein like chicken or turkey. Also, knowing the next day would require a high level of energy, I needed the calories to fuel my muscles as much as satisfy my stomach. Now, thanks to Jean, I could look forward to a good meal. As our group sat discussing the next day's agenda over a glass of wine, other mountaineers began to trickle in and take seats at the long, community-style picnic tables.

The lively conversation began to dissipate as our host arrived, bearing huge platters of steaming hot food—precisely the sort of hearty, calorie-rich grub needed by athletes who'd just finished a strenuous day of climbing. We were told my plate was coming separately. Jean, Michael, Craig, and Tim all graciously waited for my special meal to arrive. Embarrassed by what seemed an interminable delay, I encouraged my hungry teammates to dig in, but they insisted on being gentlemen. Finally, to the relief of everyone, my plate arrived. I thanked both Jean and the cook with a warm smile. Then I looked down and discovered that to prepare my "nutritious" meal she had taken the paper-thin turkey slices and deep-fried them! It was utterly unsalvageable. But, with all eyes eagerly focused on me, I had to at least pretend to be delighted. I took a tiny bite. Ugh! It was disgusting! Finally, in desperation, I nudged my plate close to Craig so he could sneak little pieces. With his stomach full of this greasy fare, I was able to proudly show off my clean plate. Later I was able to tap into my prepackaged reserves and no one was the wiser.

The next morning we were up bright and early for a day of rock climbing on the Dri Hörlini Ridge, a 1,000 foot technical traverse that sat just behind our hut. It was here that I was able to demonstrate my comfort with heights, giving Jean the confidence that I was mentally prepared for the Matterhorn. We spent the following day adhering to Jean's teaching and leadership, testing our ice axes and crampons on a nearby glacier. We were rewarded with a breathtaking view when we arrived at our lunch spot, a ridge straddling the Swiss/Italian border. While we could clearly see the surrounding Swiss Alps, the Italian side was shrouded in a layer of fog. It was eerie. We knew there was a 2,000-foot drop into a grey abyss, but we couldn't see even 20 feet below the ridgeline. Suddenly, adding to the spookiness was an enormous rockslide that echoed throughout, a noise so loud it sounded like a 747 taking off directly in front of us. It left us a little shaken, wondering where and when the next rockslide would appear.

On our final day of practice, my heart was tested as never before. Our group set out at 4:30 in the morning to ascend and traverse the Weissmies, the 13,199-foot peak that ends with a breathtaking descent down the Trift Glacier. It proved to be an optimal training spot, igniting the critical acclimatization process, challenging all our technical skills and testing our ability to endure a long, hard day. Jean was relentless about moving fast, constantly reminding us that speed would ultimately determine our success.

The trail began gradually but quickly grew increasingly steep. After several hours of hiking, the terrain turned even more vertical. Concurrently, we were coping with heightened exposure and loose rocks. I focused on my labored breath, until the burn in my legs commanded my full attention. I wanted to stop and rest, but knew I couldn't. Because I was short-roped between Jean and Craig, they would feel a tug each time I paused, and I worried that even a momentary time-out would spark Jean's ire. I was right.

He snapped, "What are you doing?"

Not wanting to tell him I felt tired, I said, "I'm just looking at the view."

"Well, don't look, *climb*!" he growled.

Even though I was rapidly approaching my threshold, I remained determined to power through the fatigue. Fortunately, most of the vertical ascent was behind us and I didn't have that much further to climb before the arduous grade leveled off. I would just have to keep moving. Ahead of us I spied a small group of climbers who had ascended the peak from the other side. Toasting one another with large cans of German ale, they were obviously reveling in the fact that they'd conquered the great Weissmies. Their enthusiasm gave me the incentive I needed. A welcome burst of reserve energy pushed me forward.

Minutes later, we too had our place on the top. We raised our ice axes in victory, sharing the mountaineering version of a "high-five" by knocking our steel-headed picks together. While the top was just the halfway point, Jean appeared to be pleased with our performance thus far. I equated his contentedness as approval of our effort, or specifically mine, given the fact that I made reasonable time. After rewarding myself with the panoramic view and a carefully calculated allotment of peanut M&Ms, it was time to make our way down the Trift Glacier, a forty-degree, crevasse-laden monster that took up nearly the entire backside of the mountain.

The previous evening, concerned about the unseasonably warm weather and threat of an avalanche, Jean had pondered if this was too risky a path for our hike out. To better assess the conditions, he consulted with a local network of mountain guides. Their word was that it still *appeared* to be in decent shape. So, after discussing it with us, he decided it was the route he wanted us to descend. We started working our way down, again moving at a fast clip and short-roped together, when we suddenly noticed climber "gridlock" in an area up ahead. We waited as Jean untied himself and went to evaluate the situation. When he rejoined our group, it soon became clear he was not happy with what he'd found. "This mountain is *not* in good shape," he sternly reported. "It looks like a critical ice bridge has collapsed and the climbers below have been forced to come up with an alternate passage. I don't know what we are going to do until I see it."

I thought to myself, "What if the revised route isn't good enough either?" If it weren't safe, we'd have to retrace seven hours of difficult climbing back to the hut. At this hour of the day, we wouldn't even arrive at our *original* starting point until well after the sun had set. The thought of this was daunting. Could my heart endure the long trek back? What if some of the towering seracs (ice cliffs) we were about to descend gave way like the ice bridge ahead? Neither proposition looked very favorable.

Jean kept moving, his face drawn and tense in the harsh sunlight. I heard him mumble, "We have to get beyond this." He then loudly commanded, "Let's move—and fast."

It was clear that Jean was stressed, as rapidly changing conditions were increasing the potential danger of what lay ahead. He pressed us to keep moving. Suddenly looming before us was our first major obstacle, a large serac that resembled a mammoth iceberg.

We figured a mountain rescue team must have already been there, because a fifteen-foot aluminum ladder had been erected straight up the ice face, which angled over a deep crevasse. Jean called out, "It looks pretty good. Tim, you and Michael go first and lead the way."

I stood at the top and watched Tim disappear as he went over the edge. Just as I was cherishing the fact that I was standing on what seemed solid ice, a disturbing cracking sound rumbled below our feet. Craig looked at Michael, who murmured, "That's not good."

From a guy who had climbed Mt. Everest on three separate occasions (he had conquered it a third time after our Kilimanjaro hike), his words were quite alarming. For me, just seeing the anxious look on Jean's face was enough to make my stomach drop.

As Tim made his way down the drop-off, Jean looked my way and said, "You and Craig wait." With his camera rolling, Michael followed Tim. He wanted to be sure to capture my precarious descent.

"Stop filming!" Jean brusquely reprimanded him.

Michael knew the danger, but he also knew a "Kodak moment." Having professionally filmed many high adventure expeditions around the world, Michael was clearly irritated by Jean's harsh directive, but nevertheless put his camera away. Like the rest of us, Michael recognized and respected Jean's leadership role and his strict emphasis on safety. The ice was melting, snow and rocks were falling. It wasn't the time or place for taking pictures.

I'm not good at waiting under such circumstances. My fear grows in direct proportion to the amount of time I'm left to sit and ponder. As I approached the edge, I looked down, but only for a glance, to see the ladder. I didn't want to see the depth of the crevasse. Craig went ahead of me, bravely inching his way down slowly, rung by rung. Once he got to the bottom and was safely over the abyss, he shouted, "You'll do great. Just go slow."

I took a deep breath, turned toward Jean, and started my way down, timidly negotiating the narrow steps in my steel spiked crampons. All I could focus on was the aluminum foothold. Moving at a snail's pace, I finally made my way to the landing. Upon reaching the bottom I said to myself, "And this is isn't even the collapsed ice bridge!"

I tried to calm myself by thinking about the combined years of mountain experience that Jean, Michael, and Tim had between them. They had sound judgment and all the survival and rescue skills necessary to get us through this. The mere fact that they were stronger than me provided comfort. My trust in them was put to the test when it came time to cross the fallen ice bridge. They told me the only way to get beyond it was to jump! It sounded so simple until I looked into the gaping crack. My heart may not be connected to my brain by nerves, but glancing into this void seemed to prove otherwise. I'm sure my heart was fully in tune with my anxiety as I felt an adrenaline rush surge through my body. Tim and Michael leapt first, followed by Craig. Craig's nearly a foot taller than me, and he barely made it! He lunged forward and soared to the other side. Immediately he turned to Jean and said, "There is no way Kelly can make it across this." As I had to go next, this was not a good thing to hear; yet there was no turning back. I was roped to Jean on one side of the crevasse, with Craig, Tim, and Michael on the other when Jean yelled to me, "Go!"

Just then, the receiving team yanked the rope. I pulled a Peter Pan type move, stretching my arms outward like wings, and using whatever flexibility I had to extend my legs as far as they could reach. During the brief moments that I flew through the air, my heart felt like it was going to jump out of my chest. For a split second, I wondered if it might be the only part of me to make it to the other side! With little room to spare, I was able to slam my ice ax into the frozen wall that towered in front of me, and then dig my crampons into the thin edge that served as the platform against the glacial mass. I cheered, "I made it!" I glanced over at Craig just in time to see a wide grin of relief fill his face.

Once we'd regrouped, Jean insisted we all rope up together to descend the next leg of the slope. Until then, Craig and I were on a short rope with Jean, while Michael and Tim were short-roped together as a separate team. The angle of the terrain pointed sharply downward causing Jean to bark out a new set of instructions. Tim responded by setting an ice screw for added protection and belayed us off of the final slippery pitch.

As the glacier gradually leveled off, our focus shifted to the intermittent crevasses that threaded the lower terrain. I looked out ahead, and noticed a significant change in the snowfield. The white velvet blanket of untouched snow that we saw above had vanished and become uneven and discolored. I was spooked, imagining with every step that the temperamental glacier was thinning and would give way at any moment. I envisioned myself breaking through the ice and landing in a freezing pool of water that would instantly petrify my blood. I was *very* motivated to get off the mountain!

We were extremely relieved when we reached the bottom and were away from the ice and rock fall line. I looked back at what we had just descended, thankful to have completed the trek without incident. Michael said, "That was every bit as tricky and treacherous as the Khumbu icefalls on Everest." The Trift Glacier stood tall, like a looming tsunami rearing up to engulf those who ventured near. Far above, I could still make out climbers who were working their way down. With the cracking ice still echoing in my ears, I was glad to once again have solid dirt under my feet.

Once our crampons were off, we proceeded another half mile, and were greeted by the site of the upper station of a high Alpine gondola. What made the welcome sight even sweeter was that it housed a small restaurant where we could grab a well-deserved drink and snack. Having trekked for about thirteen hours, the smell of food and thought of sitting were nirvana. We ate a quick meal on the sunny, open-air deck, and then dragged our tired bodies onto the lift, waiting to take us to the valley below. I felt exhausted by my sustained anxiety, yet invigorated by what we had just accomplished. Once off the tram, we headed for the train that would take us back to Zermatt.

As I waited for the train, still basking in the glow of my day's accomplishment, Jean privately turned to me and said, "You took too long today and at that pace, I don't think you will reach the top of the Matterhorn." I was blown away. All my hard-won confidence deflated. At first, I thought he was referring to someone else. After all, I had just done extremely well. But, with what had now become his usual abruptness, he looked directly at me and continued, "As hard as this day was, it was nothing compared to the Matterhorn." I felt all the energy drain out of my body. As he watched me slump, he offered a conciliatory aside, saying, "Even the best alpinists don't always summit the Matterhorn."

I remained completely taken back. What was he thinking? I was in very good shape. He knew from the beginning what he was getting himself into. Craig and I had gone over every detail of my limitations and challenges. Nonetheless, his comments suggested to me that he'd lost sight of everything that mattered—my condition, our mission, and the symbolism associated with this event.

On the train, Michael, Tim, and Jean sat about five rows behind us. I tried to maintain my composure as I told Craig what Jean had said, but I began to weep uncontrollably. I was hurt to think that we'd trained for months, come all this way, and were committed to a guide who I now felt was not going to help champion my effort. I was used to surrounding myself with people who cheered me on, which in turn motivated me to do my best. As always, Craig wrapped his arm around me and patiently listened as I vented my frustration. After I spilled my guts, he said, "I know you can do this, but it's a big climb and you need to feel confident in both your own capabilities as well as in your guide. Whatever you decide, climb or no climb, I'll support you. Either way, you need to talk to Jean as soon as we get off the train in Zermatt."

Once we arrived at the station, Craig and I waited for Michael to catch up with us. Looking for a second opinion, I pulled him aside and shared Jean's skepticism. By this point I had worked myself into a state of frenzy, and was questioning my own capabilities. Because of my trust in Michael's experience and his personal knowledge of my climbing potential and history, I desperately wanted his support. "Please be honest with me," I pleaded. "What do you think? Can I do it?" Michael immediately responded, "Kelly, I know your strength and determination—your sheer willpower makes you stronger than most mountaineers I know."

Just then, Jean and Tim approached us. My intent was to talk privately to Jean and tell him how I felt. However, my emotions got the best of me and I lost it in front of everyone. I turned to Jean and, choking through my tears, demanded, "You *have* to support me. I *know* I can make it. I want to stand on the summit more than anyone here."

Michael chimed in, "Listen Jean, if Kelly was like every other mountaineer here why would I be filming her? Why would the Associated Press be arriving to do a story about her? She's not letting her medical condition stop her and neither should you. She may not be like your other clients, but let me tell you, when push comes to shove, Kelly's strength kicks in. I've witnessed it first hand on numerous occasions and I know what she can do. She's got more determination than any other climber you'll ever lead. You've got to give her the chance to prove what she can do."

From his reaction to Michael's cheerleading speech, I could tell Jean felt bad. He thought for a moment, and then proffered a deal, saying, "I'll take you up, but if we don't get to the Solvay Hütte by noon, which is just over three-fourths of the way up, we're turning back. No resting! We rest when we get to the summit." I felt demoralized for a moment, but couldn't dwell on his wavering faith in my abilities. I knew the most important tool I had was to believe in myself, and I had just two days before we ascended the Matterhorn to rebuild my shaky self-confidence.

As Jean wandered off, Tim reached out to me with his own words of encouragement. He said, "Just so you know, during my training as an aspiring guide, Jean was known among the students as the "morale buster." It takes a lot to gain his respect, and he prides himself on being painfully honest. In fact, today was the very first time I ever received a compliment from him, which would not have happened if you had not held your own." I thought to myself, "now I have one more motivation to get to the top of the Matterhorn—I would show my resilience and *earn* Jean's respect.

CHAPTER 13

Full Circle

WITH one day to rest, Craig and I strolled around Zermatt, recalling fond memories of our anniversary celebration there in 1992. Adjacent to the church in the town's main square is a small graveyard. On our previous visit, we'd found it quaint and charming. This time, the headstones, many marking climbers who had met their demise on the surrounding peaks, took on a rather unnerving significance. Several of the stones were, in their depiction of brave, dramatic ends, as impressive as works of art as they were as memorials. One that caught my eye was for a seventeen-year-old mountaineer who died while climbing the Breithorn. It featured an ice ax, mounted crossways on the tombstone, accompanied by the simple but powerful statement, "I chose to climb." Another was adorned with an image of a crucified Christ dressed as a climber, with ax and rope hanging from his body. Intriguing as the stones were, neither Craig nor I, knowing where we were headed the very next day, wanted to dwell too long on the Alps-related accidents that resulted in their erection.

We strolled on through the bustling town square, clustered with crowded restaurants, cafes, and bars wedged between stores flaunting posh outdoor apparel, Swiss goods and fine jewelry. A few discrete peeks at the price tags revealed that even a pair of sock liners was enough to put a dent in our carefully planned budget. Instead, I stuck to window-shopping, while Craig happily grazed among the sausage and ice cream stands in an effort to bulk up for the challenging days ahead.

Later, when all the stores closed for their afternoon siesta, we went looking for a lunch spot and came across a memorial plaque to Ed Whymper, the first man to summit the Matterhorn. It was both daunting and inspiring to know that Ed had failed seven times before finally making a successful ascent in 1865. As we walked on, we continued to be amused by the charming streets and alleyways. Because no cars are allowed, the town is crowded with pedestrians and horse-drawn carriages. Naturally, the mountaineers dotted amongst the tourists caught our eyes, particularly if they were proudly sporting signature Swiss climbing attire, including backpacks, ice axes, and traditional short trousers that resembled the famed lederhosen. We carefully examined their faces for any hints of triumph or defeat.

Along our walk, we passed a few, weathered timber barns that made us feel we were stepping back in time. A few shacks, carefully propped up on stone pedestals, were actually leaning and looked ready to collapse. The sight of it conjured alarming images of the surrounding Alps, where falling rocks had, thanks to the long, hot summer, become a significant hazard.

Ever full of ideas, Craig made a spur-of-the-moment suggestion. "Let's find the trail and retrace where we hiked eleven years ago." After a little searching, we located the path, winding up a steep grade on the outskirts of town. We'd made it only a little way up when darkening skies unleashed a torrent of rain and lightening, forcing us to retreat. Focusing on the positive, we decided it was a good omen, indicating that we no longer belonged in the shadow of the Matterhorn, but on the famed peak itself.

Scurrying back to our hotel, we tried not to focus on the daunting climb awaiting us, instead concentrating on packing and a final tally of our equipment. The next morning I awoke with my usual belly full of butterflies. But as soon as I saw the hotel's lavish breakfast spread the butterflies were replaced by greedy hunger. Their morning offering would delight the fussiest foodies, and caused even me, the most careful of eaters, to overindulge. The enticing buffet included smoked salmon, wholegrain breads, eggs, Muesli and a mountain of oranges for fresh-squeezed juice. It was heavenly to know I could eat to my heart's content, gorging on nutritious food that would fuel my strength throughout the day. Settling into a window table, we looked out at ominous gunmetal skies and swollen clouds that hinted at heavy rain. The magnificent smorgasbord wasn't enough to keep my mind from the weather and accompanying frigid temperatures. I only hoped the threatening clouds would dissipate, leaving bright skies for the next day, our summit day. Downing a final sip of coffee, I told Craig I was now charged and ready to go. Sensing my anxiousness, Craig said, "Coffee may get you going, but it's your steadfast commitment that keeps you going."

We collected the belongings we'd need for the next few nights and met up with Jean and Tim, who were both anxious to get moving. With groaning packs, the five of us walked a few blocks to the Schwartzee cable car lift which would take us to the starting point of our climb, a trail that would then lead to the Hörnli Hütte. There were no crowds waiting for the lift, so Craig and I snagged our own gondola, delighted to have some last-minute privacy. We snuggled close together for the short twelve-minute ride. I expected to remain focused on the mountain ahead, but instead became transfixed by the tiny chalets that dotted the landscape below, imaging a simple life in such serene and majestic surroundings. Below, everything was lush and green, but looming above were steep faces of gray rock, ice, and snow. Cows grazing peacefully in the valley reminded me of the greatest of all Matterhorn guides, the late Ulrich Inderbinenold. I admired his lifelong insistence on moving at a pace that was slow and deliberate, but also purposeful. He must have been doing something right—the man ascended this magnificent peak a reported 370 times!

We reached the top of the lift and began our two-and-a-half-hour hike to the Hütte. There was no time to linger, as the clouds were about to burst. Midway up, it began to rain, prompting all of us to cover our packs. The hike was along a dirt path, fairly gentle in grade, graduating to sections of rocky, steep steps that became increasingly slippery as the skies opened. I pitied the poor climbers on the sheer slopes of the mountain.

The Hörnli Hütte is positioned close to the foot of the mountain near the approach of the climb. From the outside it is similar to many of the chalets in town, stucco-framed with wooden window boxes and an open deck. Anxious to get out of our damp jackets, we hurried inside and were immediately greeted by Cedric, Craig's guide for summit day. Jean and Cedric headed out to the approach of the climb to assess the trail condition and the weather. Jean had told us the entire next day was contingent on it clearing, as stormy weather would make the climb considerably more dangerous. I heard the skepticism that had so rattled me earlier in the trip creep into Jean's voice, and dreaded the thought of spending an entire day waiting for the weather to improve while listening to his dire rumblings.

The inside of the hut, designed purely for functionality, was just a place to sleep and eat. Because of my necessary obsession with germs, I was less concerned about decorating touches than cleanliness, and was delighted to see how neat and well-scrubbed the space was kept. In accordance with traditional hut etiquette, we parked our boots near the front door. When Jean returned from playing "wetter" (weather) man, he talked to the innkeeper who directed him to our beds. As we made our way to the top floor, I grabbed a pair of hut slippers off the rack, happy to find not only a left and right, but also a pair that was close to my size. I was expecting dorm rooms like we'd had at the Almageller Hütte, adorned with wooden sleeping shelves with one big pad for everyone to share. Instead, the six of us were given a room to ourselves. Although our space was a cozy 10 x 10 at best, we each had the luxury of our own bunk. The toilet, more of a seat over a pit, was a short walk down the hall. In spite of the offensive smell, I was happy just to have it indoors so I didn't have to brave the cold. The room was outfitted with the standard assortment of pads, blankets, and pillows. As an aside, I continue to be impressed by how diligently and restfully climbers fold and stow the shared bedclothes, just as they are asked to do, before their predawn departures.

We had some free time before dinner, so Craig and I, knowing pre-climb nerves would likely keep us awake most of the night, decided to catch a quick nap. I nestled up against him, my head cradled in his shoulder, my favorite place to escape from the hardships of reality (climb or no climb!), secure in the knowledge that I'm safe, protected and, most important of all, loved. It seemed we'd just nodded off when delicious aromas drifted upward, beckoning us to dinner. Craig and I spotted Michael, Cedric, and Tim, who had secured a table within the crowded dining room. The hot meal was simple but full of flavor, as they always seem to be in the mountains. Nerves didn't seem to be impeding anyone's appetite, mine included. As dessert was being served, I glanced around. The room may have been sparse, but it was overflowing with warmth and charm, thanks to the climbers, converging in this tiny space from all corners of the globe, who glowed with energetic camaraderie.

Because most climbers start as early as 4:00 A.M., everyone was expected to turn in by nine at night. Jean, always a step ahead of the crowd, bellowed "time for bed!" I eagerly obliged. Well aware of my need for middle-of-the-night bathroom runs, I chose a lower bunk and Craig climbed in the one adjacent. I was just about to fall asleep when I caught the overpowering scent of Vicks VapoRub as it followed someone into the room. My view blocked by the upper bunk and hanging clothes, all I could see was an unfamiliar pair of skinny legs. Sure enough it was Cedric and, after I repositioned myself to look up at him, I could see him rubbing the mentholated balm below his nose to clear his sinuses. Immediately, alarm bells went off in my head. He must have a cold! With a hugely challenging climb just hours away, here I was stuck in a closet-sized room with a guy who was about to spread sinister germs all over the place. Great! On top of Jean's dire weather forecast, now I could add the threat of a virulent virus to my nighttime fears. I pulled a jacket over my head and tried to get some sleep. Around midnight, I woke up and headed for the bathroom. Cedric was quietly sleeping, and Jean whispered, "The sky's are clear—we're going for it. Get some sleep." All my worrying was for naught!

Our 4:00 A.M. wakeup call came abruptly. The hut keepers laid out a predawn breakfast for the day's climbers;

nothing fancy—just dry bread, butter, cheese, jam and coffee, hardly the gourmet spread we'd enjoyed at the hotel. Finally, we'd reached the morning that Jean had been drilling us so hard for on the Weismeiss. I was determined to show him what I was made of. After one glimpse at his dour expression, I avoided looking at him, instead focusing on his clipped commands as he inspected my clothes and equipment. As I clumsily struggled with the fastener of my helmet, he snapped, "Give it to me, I'll do it." Michael was capturing this showdown with his camera, so I managed to crack a smile that suggested I found Jean's authoritativeness cute or fun. But, deep down I was thinking, "I have *how many* hours of this ahead of me?" Jean then tied his rope to my harness like an umbilical cord and hauled me out the door into the darkness. It was a relief to start the trail, and to do so on time. I needed all the points I could score, and knowing we'd kept to the taskmaster's schedule was an excellent start. I am glad we didn't dally, because a stream of climbers with flickering headlamps were already scrambling to position themselves ahead of the notorious first bottleneck at the base of the wall. Jean said, "The first fixed rope will determine our entire day. If we fall behind, we'll be waiting all the way up and we won't make it."

A line of twenty climbers had gathered, waiting their turn to ascend the first pitch. When it was time for our team to go, Jean ascended the fixed rope and quickly scurried out of sight onto a ledge somewhere above. As I reached for the rope, I started slipping on a bank of ice that lined the foot of the wall. It took me by surprise how difficult it was to gain any sort of traction and get off the ground. I rocked back and forth for what seemed an eternity, without moving up an inch. I knew if I didn't move soon, I'd been facing the ire of the long line of climbers behind me. Just as I was starting to feel clumsy and powerless, I felt a welcome tug from above. Jean pulled the rope taught, providing the friction and stabilization I needed to move up. Having made it through the first obstacle, my concern shifted from *getting* ahead, to *staying* ahead.

For the next forty-five minutes, I could sense the growing steepness of the mountain, including the space filled drop-offs that lurked in the dark. Only the sounds of my heavy breathing and beating heart filled the emptiness. Just before the star-filled night sky made way for the first glimmer of dawn's light, I suffered a moment's panic, thinking, "My God, what have I gotten myself into?" My 4:00 A.M. coffee had kicked in and my heart seemed to be working well. Still, every single step seemed so labored in comparison to Jean's absurdly fast pace. I could hardly catch my breath. To top it off, scrambling on the craggy terrain required me to pay close attention to my footing, a not-so-easy task at such a swift clip. As much as I worked to stay focused, it was not enough. I had to find something small to look forward to. I focused on the weak ray of battery-powered light emanating from my helmet, knowing the real thing would soon replace it. "Yes," I reassured myself, "the warmth of the sun will give me the extra energy I so desperately need."

Slogging up a particularly steep crag, I heard Michael's voice, sounding as if it was coming from somewhere in front of me. As soon as I caught up with him, he could see "struggle" written all over my face. Without missing a beat, he said, "You are doing great—you're my hero." Here was a guy who had hauled excruciatingly heavy camera gear to the top of Mt. Everest, yet was sensitive enough to know I was in desperate need of an emotional boost. His heartfelt willingness to stretch the truth and suggest we were climbing equals proved what a true gentleman he is. And, it was precisely what I needed to hear!

It was one of the most beautiful, and certainly the most welcome, sunrises I'd ever seen, and it *did* ignite my inner fire. My heart was performing exceptionally well and my pace was impressive, even by my own standards! Still, it wasn't long before I was in the doghouse once again. Jean was steadily navigating the ridge and, because I was short-roped to him, I was instructed to follow directly behind. I would make an effort to stay high, but felt safer a little below, enabling me to use the sharp stone ridge for my hands.

Jean caught me a second time, then demanded in a harsh, scolding tone, "Stay on the ridge. Not right or left—but *on the ridge!*" I understood the theory of gravity, and knew that falling rocks posed a grave concern to climbers below, but it still seemed less dangerous than balancing the narrow ridge with steep drops on both sides. Wishing to avoid further abuse, I vowed I'd do nothing else to arouse his wrath.

We approached a spot where, because of a rock tower that had collapsed a few weeks earlier, the route had been detoured. A fat fixed rope, like the one we'd used at the beginning of the climb, was positioned to guide climbers over the unstable debris. It was our introduction to "climber congestion," giving me new appreciation for Jean's nagging desire for speed.

Jean pushed up against the bottlenecked climbers, each anxious to be next on the only available rope, and loudly barked, "Move! Get out of our way." Not bothering to wait for a response, he forced me right in front, brushing the other climbers aside. I said nothing but thought to myself "*how rude!*" It reminded me of road rage in bumper-to-bumper L.A. traffic. Then it became apparent that Jean wasn't the only guide maneuvering to overtake the rope. Each of the equally experienced local guides was behaving just as aggressively. All that mattered was the job at hand—getting their clients to the top of the mountain and back down again. Manners were for polite dinner parties, not the Matterhorn.

Jean's relentless speed kept us at a good clip that found me passing other climbers. Typically it's me who gets lapped. As we continued the mad scramble, I could see we were approaching an important milestone, the Solvay Hütte, located about three-quarters of the way up. Remembering Jean's dictate that if we didn't make it there by noon he'd turn us around, I snuck a peek at my watch and discovered we were nearly two hours ahead of schedule. I now knew I had a real chance of making the summit and fulfilling my dream!

The Solvay Hütte, nestled on the shoulder of the ridge, was designed as an emergency bivouac, a closet-sized shelter that can squeeze six to eight climbers if they get caught in bad weather or get delayed by going off route. While its rustic wood structure appears inviting, it actually emits a rather foul smell; the rear exterior wall doubles as a convenient bathroom stop for many passersby. The stench provided me all the incentive I needed to keep moving.

As I paused to catch my breath, Craig and Cedric took the opportunity to move in front of Jean. The short rest caused my heart to slow, resulting in typical grief when I resumed. My breathing was labored and I couldn't help but move slowly. By now Jean was fully aware of my condition, yet he still appeared to be having a hard time remembering the challenges I faced. Because I had been doing so well before I stopped, when I struggled to get going again, I could tell by the look on his face that he thought I wasn't pushing myself hard enough. I was so out of breath I couldn't say a word. Finally, he stopped and extracted a glucose tablet from his pocket. I laughed to myself, thinking, "He really does not get it! It's not my blood sugar, it's my heart!" Out of sheer frustration, I took it, despite his soiled gloves, ate it, and tried to stay focused. Just when I thought the slope couldn't possibly get any steeper, the ascent seemed to pitch further skyward. Suddenly, someone from above yelled out "rock," causing us all to hug the mountain. I felt a sense of relief after a cannonball-sized stone whizzed over my helmet, smashing a few feet behind me before cascading off the ridge far below. Guides had warned us that falling rocks were this climb's biggest danger, and the leading cause of death on the mountain. If I had any doubt before, that near miss drove the point home.

The territorial "guide wars" seemed to intensify at the fixed rope areas. The outbursts became increasingly more plentiful as the ridge tapered and snow and ice made exposed rocks slippery, slowing the process of all the climbers. As we neared the celebrated snow-capped peak, we paused to put on our crampons. As much as I welcomed the spikes' added traction, careful maneuvering was required as other dangers presented themselves. At one point, I was badgered into hurrying up a rope and, looking up, all I saw were razor-sharp crampons hovering inches from my face. One simple slip or misstep would have resulted in deep facial lacerations, which weren't anywhere near as frightening to me as the inevitable infection that would accompany the gashes.

It was late morning as we made our way up the final leg of the steep icy slope. There was now more sky than rock ahead, which invigorated me to push on. The crisp, clean air and cobalt blue sky felt to me like a natural incubator, protecting my system from any risk. The strong beat of my heart reflected how terrific the rest of my body felt. The idea that I was in any way physically limited seemed preposterous.

After five-and-a-half straight hours of scaling nearly 5,000 vertical feet, we were about to be rewarded for all the intense training and hard work. My emotions shifted into overdrive as we approached our ultimate destination. I turned and waited for Craig who, along with Cedric, was now trailing a short distance behind. Naturally, we wanted to summit at the same time.

Jean carefully made his way along the Italian side of the ridge, while I hugged the snow-encrusted Swiss side. He then suddenly stopped and turned to look at me, prompting me to ask what I already knew, "Is this it?" As Jean confirmed that we were indeed standing on the peak's highest point, I threw my arms into the air in triumph, drawing accolades from all those who had participated in this momentous event. Jean then leaned over the invisible international border and gave me a congratulatory hug, then followed European custom by planting a kiss on each of my cheeks. More important, he acknowledged that I had performed extremely well. There was no doubt he was impressed, as I had proven myself to be a worthy alpinist.

My mind continued to race with excitement. I could tell from the look on Craig's face that he was equally overcome. Given our deep personal ties to this mountain, I knew this achievement was as important to him as it was to me. We leaned toward one other and shared a long, warm hug that simultaneously embraced our past, present, and future.

Craig looked down the north side of the slope and pointed out to our team the area where the two of us had been hiking eleven years earlier, mere months before I was first diagnosed with my heart condition. I could easily imagine people far below in the valley, peering up as we had all those years ago, awestruck by the intimidating grandeur of where we now stood. Craig was too choked up to talk, but words weren't necessary. The feeling of success was so intense it could remain unspoken. Silently, we reveled in the knowledge that our lives had come full circle.

Breaking into Craig's and my reflective mood, Jean said, "Look at the view." We'd been so wrapped up in our private moment of triumph that we'd failed to fully appreciate the spectacular panorama. Craig and I straddled one foot in Italy and the other in Switzerland as we drank in the intoxicating magic of the seemingly endless horizon. Finally, something other than my heart took my breath away.

Jean pointed out a few of the famous landmarks, including the Saint Bernard statue we had passed just below the summit and the iron cross on the Italian side of the ridge which commemorates lives lost on the mountain. It seems I am constantly reminded of how fragile, and how precious, life is.

Looking into the distance, we could see Mt. Blanc and Mt. Rosa as well as some threatening weather that was slowly making its way toward us from the southeast. Recognizing that our time at the summit was limited, Craig rallied the team to share in our tradition of blowing bubbles. And, adhering to a more personal tradition, he presented me with my fifth mountain charm; a beautifully contoured gold keepsake in the distinctive shape of what was now my *favorite* peak! The charm clearly detailed the steep north face ridge we had just ascended, and was crowned with a pave of diamonds that represented the ice and snow. Once again, I was breathless.

Craig then announced he had a couple more surprises. He pulled out a necklace that TJ had given to him to pre-

sent to me when we reached the summit. It bore the inspirational inscription, *climb as high as your dreams*. It was
friends like TJ who, thanks to their unflagging support and
encouragement, had enabled me to do precisely that.

Craig presented a very special note and wish wand
from our local ranger friend, Larry Sweet, a staunch supporter of our mission to build awareness of organ donation. About a year earlier, we'd learned of Larry's own
tragic connection to heart disease. Larry's nineteen-year-
old son, Brian, had unexpectedly died as a result of sudden
cardiac arrest. When Craig told him of our Matterhorn
climb, Larry gave Craig a wish wand so we could blow
bubbles from the summit in honor of his son. Larry also
gave him a copy of his son's eulogy, added a note stating,
"Brian understood teamwork and friendship and how
the two lead to success while representing success in and
of themselves." It was a wonderful sentiment that Craig
and I could both relate to.

Finally, as if my heart couldn't swell any larger, Craig
gave me a touching note from Reg and Maggie Green.
The Greens are well known organ donor advocates whom
Craig had reached out to shortly after my climb up Mt.
Whitney. Not knowing our donor family at the time, he
wanted to express his appreciation to a family who had
donated organs, and relay that my recent accomplishment
was a result of the benevolence of people like them. Coin-
cidentally, just one day later, Craig received that fateful first
call from Greta. With the Greens note was a wish wand
and photo of their seven-year-old son, Nicholas, whose
organs were donated to Italian families after his untimely
death during a 1994 family vacation in Europe. Reg and
Maggie's message, intended to offer hope for those waiting
for life-saving organs, encouraged prospective recipients,
"to have the strength in mind and body to hang on until

one comes." Ironically, the photo—the last picture taken of Nicholas before he died—showed him standing in front of the Matterhorn!

Our various rituals completed, Jean reminded us it was now time to depart, ominously observing that, "the most difficult portion is still ahead." As I looked around, the blue sky was rapidly filling with dark clouds, which would soon be dusting us with snow. After such an emotional summit experience, it was difficult to refocus on navigating my body down the steep, slippery slopes. Looking at the perilous drop we were about to face, my thoughts turned to Ed Whymper's first successful summit and the four members of his team who perished on the way down. My euphoria was evaporating quickly.

While the rest of us began our backward descent, Michael remained behind with Tim for what was supposed to be only a few extra minutes to send text and photos to Explorer's Web, which had been monitoring our climb on the Internet. Thanks to this cleverly crafted website, friends, family, and fellow climbing enthusiasts around the world were able to share our adventure in real time.

It wasn't long before the peak disappeared inside a shroud of white, causing Jean to command that we move faster to stay ahead of the afternoon storm. Michael was having trouble getting satellite reception at the top. As such, he and Tim were delayed for over an hour, and got caught in the snow that followed shortly thereafter. Though I was hustling as quickly as I safely could, I sensed another dark cloud looming—one formed of Jean's impatience and frustration. Craig and Cedric tried to keep pace by repelling off-route in a few areas that were parallel to our position. The sparks flying off Craig's crampons scraping against the rock indicated the aggressive speed at which they were descending.

Pushing with all my might, fueled only by a handful of M&Ms and another of Jean's glucose tablets, I spotted the Hörnli Hütte far below. I could now clearly see the section we'd ascended in the dark at the beginning of our climb. No wonder I'd felt defeated and in such desperate need of the encouraging words Michael had then provided. The sheer grade of the route was terrifying.

As I took my final step off the official "rock," I came face to face with a daunting plaque that had been obscured in darkness on the way up. It was a warning erected by the parents and friends of a young man who died while attempting to climb this famous peak. It was spelled out in four different languages:

> *Fallen in this Wall. He had neither knowledge of mountaineering nor adequate equipment. His parents and friends wish to remind not to attempt climbing the Matterhorn without experience, as mountain and weather conditions may change rapidly.*

Those words indeed reminded me how fortunate I was to have such skilled and seasoned teammates, and made me think that perhaps covering this treacherous section under a cloak of darkness wasn't such a bad thing!

By the time we arrived at the hut, we'd been on the move for nearly thirteen hours. I was overjoyed to be back on level ground! We immediately removed all our damp layers of clothing and refueled with hot tea and snacks. Jean settled into a table already occupied by a group of guides. They looked like typical businessmen meeting up for an after work drink to share the day's events. Jean talked the most, obviously regaling the others' with a tale they were anxious to hear. My back was to their table, and I pretended not to notice the eyes looking my way. I understood their curiosity. After all, there weren't too many remaining firsts on the Matterhorn. As the guides stood up to return to their clients, Jean came over, gave me a hug and said, "Your performance was exceptionally good." For the first time in days, the intimidating, authoritarian Jean was gone and the kind, funny man I'd liked so much when we first met was back. I returned his warm smile and, after a moment's reflection, said, "I would do it all over again, and with you!" I had come to learn that his leadership style is precisely what's required for a challenge this great, and was thrilled to know that he'd eventually come to believe in my ability and determination.

Our original plan was to rest only briefly at the hut, then hike back down to the lift that would take us to the village. However, after waiting for Michael and Tim, we missed the evening's last lift. It would be too much for our exhausted legs to endure another several hours hike to the village, so Jean suggested we stay the night. Fortunately, the hut could accommodate us. As the darkening sky grew increasingly ominous, we heard the sound of a rescue helicopter. We waited inside as Air Zermatt gracefully set down to drop off a rescued woman at the hut. I couldn't help but be reminded of the disconcerting mortality rate on this mountain. I offered a silent prayer to the skilled pilots who, thanks to their diligence and bravery, made it safer for all of us to pursue our towering dreams.

Early the next morning, we made our way back to our hotel in time for breakfast. We were all a bit grubby, but the hotel staff was long since used to bedraggled climbers. After breakfast, Craig and I hurried to our room, eager for a hot shower and a warm, cozy bed. Michael told us he was going to take a stroll into town, and we promised to meet up with him later for drinks and dinner. I was thoroughly enjoying my peaceful rest, when Michael rang our room, urging us to join him earlier than planned. "Come meet me in town for a final photo," he insisted. "The light is perfect."

As Craig and I walked down the street, we saw Michael's camera pointed toward us. "Keep walking, like you don't see me," he said. Of course, I couldn't resist the chance to do something silly, so I wiggled my hips in an attempt to act playfully goofy. When I turned around to see Michael's reaction, I was shocked to see he wasn't alone. Standing right next to him were my mom and dad! While I was hamming it up, Craig had darted into their hotel to collect them. I couldn't believe that he had come up with yet another way to tug at my heartstrings. We all shared a magical evening, my parents hanging on every word as we shared details of our latest high-flying adventure, and me growing more than a little misty about Craig's endless thoughtfulness and relishing the company of my two Carols—mom beside me and my donor never far from my heart.

Craig and I had agreed that if we were successful in our summit attempt, we'd reward ourselves with a helicopter ride around the mountain. So, the following morning, just hours before our departure, we found ourselves preparing for one last look at our favorite peak. The clear sky was bright blue as we boarded the small, red chopper and swiftly made our way toward the mountain. Appearing as if it were anxiously awaiting our return, the Matterhorn came into full and splendid view. Awed as I was by the mountain's majesty, it was hard not to reflect back to when another pilot made a whimsical gesture over Disneyland's replica Matterhorn in an effort to steady my frail and erratic heart. Suddenly, past and present blurred then seamlessly blended as the pilot banked sharply to offer a limitless view of what had become my symbol of hope.

CHAPTER 14

Straight through
the Heart

DURING an arduous and exhausting activity, when suffering is at its peak, its quite common to question your sanity about having voluntarily subjected yourself to such torture. But a new type of madness sets in during the final steps of a successful climb. Even before the rope is untied and your boots are off, dreams of new challenges overpower your body's aches. Though I had no desire to reconquer the Matterhorn, I began planning a new adventure. I never aim to outdo a previous achievement, but rather my goal becomes finding projects that will facilitate my growth as a climber. Craig and I thrive on conceiving plans that challenge not just our bodies but also our spirits.

Inspiration came from a most unexpected source. In 2004 I ran across an old email from David Roberts, a twenty-two-year-old Australian, congratulating us on our Kilimanjaro climb. He had included a photo of himself smiling atop New Zealand's Mt. Aspiring, along with the suggestion that we add this mountain to our list. Dave had climbed the icy peak back in 2001 to raise money for bone marrow transplant research. With a name like Mt. Aspiring, located in one of the most glorious natural settings on earth, and the challenge of sharpening our alpine skills, this mountain immediately eclipsed all others. Further research revealed that New Zealand had one of the lowest organ donor rates in the developed world. This decided my mission. After emailing Dave again to learn more about his experience, his family sadly informed us he'd lost his bout with Non-Hodgkins Lymphoma. He was only twenty-five.

Mt. Aspiring, indeed the entire Aspiring National Park, owes its dramatic beauty to steeply pitched peaks jutting into the bowl of blue skies. Resembling the Swiss Alps, Mt. Aspiring is known as the Matterhorn of the South.

In the New Zealand summer of 2005, our expedition was underway. The first leg began with a helicopter flight to the base of the park's glacier. The noisy journey, hugging the terrain while buzzing upward toward the icecap, felt nothing short of exhilarating. After a quick drop off onto the Bonar Glacier, the helicopter disappeared. Nothing but a white blanket of snow surrounded us. Roping up, we "tramped" quickly to the Colin Todd hut, our refuge for the next few days.

After claiming our sleeping area in the hut, we took a short test hike to get a sense of the conditions on Mt. Aspiring. The stability of the snow would determine if it was safe to climb. When the snow becomes too soft, the mountain's slopes collapse, causing climbers to fall. In fact, just a few days before our planned start, a twenty-two-year-old climber slipped and died while descending the lower ramp of the mountain. Determining that conditions were still too dangerous, the group decided to put Mt. Aspiring off for a day, and climb the adjacent Mt. Rolling Pin instead. Though not as distinct as Mt. Aspiring, it is a one-day glacier ascent from the hut and back, and offers a unique technical challenge we were eager to experience.

This excursion was not without its moment of heart-pounding drama. During a steep forty-five-degree exposed pitch with crevassed fraught glaciers below, I suffered an untimely drop in blood pressure, bringing on nausea and dizziness, and causing me to nearly faint. Because the exposure loomed perilously before us, Craig stuck close behind me. He grabbed my jacket collar, forced me tight against the slope, and braced me from a potentially deadly fall. Fearing my tethered rope could take the whole group down, Craig yelled for our guide Nick to freeze in place just as he was ascending the crux of the pitch above. After five very long minutes, my symptoms subsided and I managed to resume climbing. Despite the incident, and a few frayed nerves, we capped the ridge, making for a successful and, more important, safe climb.

Fortunate to have a spectacular day for our Mt. Rolling Pin ascent, we held out hope that the temperature would drop. If so, the snow would harden and we could climb Mt. Aspiring the next day. We woke up at 2:00 A.M. and got dressed in all our layers in preparation for an alpine start, only to learn that Nick had determined that the snow conditions still remained too dangerous. It was time to reevaluate our goal. My mission was to build local awareness of organ donation and change death statistics, not to become one myself! Our bid to climb Mt. Aspiring had ended.

After a grueling, two-day hike out over massive glaciers and through steep, thick forest and cold rivers, we finally made it back to civilization. In celebration of our safe return, Craig presented me with my sixth charm, a beautiful depiction of Mt. Aspiring. Though we didn't stand on that actual peak, the charm became a poignant reminder that the trip was not a failure. After all, we *had* climbed a peak in Mt. Aspiring National Park. Looking at the charm and reflecting on the experience, I realized we'd accomplished what we set out to do—to bring attention to our cause. The act of "aspiring to make a difference" represents success in and of itself. Still, I do *aspire* to return some day and make another attempt at the mountain; but my ultimate hope is for a New Zealand heart transplant recipient to be the first one to make the climb.

There wasn't much time to dwell on our New Zealand sojourn, as we needed to train for what was going to be our most intimidating climb of all. The idea came about while talking to friends about our past adventures. They asked if I had ever considered climbing El Capitan in Yosemite, California. In particular, had I heard about its famous heart? Craig and I were very familiar with El Capitan's epic 3,000-foot sheer stone face, the largest granite wall in the world, yet we didn't realize that its southwest wall had a subtle yet clearly visible natural formation in the shape of a heart. It seemed an auspicious choice for our next climb.

Despite all the notable mountains I had successfully summated, this sort of technical climb represented a totally different experience. At such heights, fear of exposure wasn't merely worrisome; it was downright terrifying.

Craig and I had first visited Yosemite Valley nearly two decades earlier. I was awestruck by the magnitude of the surrounding glacial cut walls. Equally amazing to me was the thought that there were people brave and skilled enough to climb those walls. From the safe vantage point of the valley below, I couldn't imagine how anyone could manage to hold on, let alone scale the massive stone. Hanging in midair with nothing beneath my feet to support me struck me as the very definition of insecurity. Upon examining the situation more closely, I realized my own experience proved me wrong. Support, I'd learned, doesn't always come from below. It can come from above or, in my case, from the donor's heart that beats within. With this in mind, I knew my destiny was written all over the heart route's walls.

To learn as much as I could about the climb, I turned to Bob, one of the guides we had done some training with in Joshua Tree, who had made the ascent years earlier. Bob no longer climbed big walls. Still, he remained connected to other guides in the area. He convinced me that with enough training, I could pull it off. Pull it off would be the operative word. In addition to the traditional Class 5 rock climbing we had done to train for the Matterhorn, this involved Class 6 or "aid" climbing. Using this method, the climber uses a jumar (often referred to as an "ascender"), a mechanical device that attaches to the rope. The device slides up and grips the rope as downward force is applied. The climber also uses a pair of Étrier—foot loops made of webbing used as a makeshift ladder. Hand over hand, legs in stirrups, I would literally be pulling myself up the rope. In addition to preparing me for the climb's physical demands and teaching me the fundamentals of big wall rope management, the rigorous training served to test my nerves and my tolerance for heights. Full of a lifetime of climbing wisdom, Bob reminded me that there are many skilled rock climbers who start big walls, panic, and bail. His comment sounded all too familiar from our Matterhorn experience. While it may have been a stumbling block for other people, I firmly resolved to not let it stand in my way.

The wall has a fascinating history. Numerous climbers discovered the routes. The very first ascent happened as recently as 1958. A climber with the rather august, presidential name Warren Harding, spent months working on sections of it and, in his final attempt to do it in one piece, spent weeks living on the wall while inching his way to the top. As I read the stories of Harding, and the other El Cap pioneers, I could relate to their adventurous desire to conquer the seemingly impossible.

More than seventy big wall routes have been established on El Capitan's southwest and southeast faces, though many of these are variations connecting two or more of the earlier established routes. Several of these routes have auspicious names, reminiscent of the era in which courageous people conquered them. The 1950s and early 1960s climbs have more conservative names such as "The Nose." By the time the 1970s rolled around, the names became distinctly psychedelic. I'm willing to bet that the climbers who first charted Mescalito, Magic Mushroom, and Tangerine Trip were enjoying "trips" that weren't entirely physical. These amusing and quirky names brought me comfort; I wouldn't be the first druggie to climb El Capitan! Although these climbers were extremely talented even by today's standards, I better understood their mindset when I was told, "There were some people you would never climb with on drugs, and some who you would *only* climb with if they were on drugs."

The operation of climbing El Capitan, as with all mountains, begins with an unnerving sensation. But, calmed and reassured by the wonderful symbolism of following the heart route, I embraced the adventure as an incredible opportunity. The indelible stone heart embossed on El Capitan's face would act as a beacon, hopefully drawing people to our message. Aid style climbing, ascending the ropes, seemed especially metaphoric. I envisioned that every time I pulled myself up on the rope, I would be tugging the public's heartstrings, and hoped my feat would build not just awareness of organ donation but increase participation.

To further help drive my point home, the Central California Blood Center stepped into action, organizing a blood drive and touting the state's new online donor registry. We hoped that by sharing my day-to-day progress via satellite webcasts and in regional newspapers, my climb would indeed become this beacon, a springboard to increased registration. Commemorative t-shirts were also created and distributed to would-be blood donors and registrants, complements of our long time sponsor, Oakley. On the front was a black and white photo of El Cap with an isolated splash of red that highlighted the symbol of our climb. *Exercise Your Heart, Be a Blood and Organ Donor*, was the message on the front, along with the theme of our climb, *Straight through the Heart.*

Craig and I put together a strong, qualified team. Michael was on board once again to document our climb. New to the group were Kevin Thaw, who would be Michael's rigger, and Yosemite mountain guides Scott Stowe and Ken Yager. Ken and Scott were seasoned big wall climbers and, combined, had scaled El Capitan more than one hundred times. Scott would serve as our team leader, meaning he would climb first. As such, he would use various forms of protection (cam, hook, piton), jamming or hammering them into cracks to hold his weight as he ascended. This process involves intense focus, precision, and skill. If the gear is not solidly placed and blows free, the climber can quickly become airborne and suffer a long fall. A big wall is not a place for sloppy work. Even the most seasoned climbers have an innate fear of falling, which conveniently serves to keep them alive.

Our biggest challenge was to pay close attention to the puzzling network of ropes and keep them all in order. I needed to be sure that I was always properly tied in. Letting my guard down for even the briefest of moments could send me, or one of my teammates, plummeting to the bottom. Also, knowing and executing my role, being accountable for all my gear and being intimately familiar with my partner's roles all remained crucial for a successful ascent. A climb of this magnitude was a team effort of the highest order. If one person failed, we all failed.

Craig and I had trained extensively throughout California: at Yosemite, Joshua Tree, Idyllwild, and Taquitz, as well as Moab in Utah and at the Gunk's in New York. We also arranged several outings with Scott; honing our jumaring skills and joining him on an overnight practice climb with conditions similar to those we'd face on El Cap. It was an excellent opportunity to test our knowledge and measure our ability to match his style and rhythm. Each person has his or her own unique personality and way of climbing. It is extremely helpful to witness such idiosyncrasies firsthand prior to any big undertaking. We didn't want to encounter any surprises.

As team leader, Scott chose the specific crack lines we would ascend, which would take us "straight through the heart" and then up the Salathe wall route. However, just days before we left for the climb, he changed his mind and suggested we instead move from the heart over to the Muir wall route. It is sustained, steep, and featureless, which makes it extremely difficult to free climb. Therefore, nearly the entire route needs to be aided. His decision confused me, and I asked, "Why the most difficult route? Do we really need to make this any more of a challenge than it already is?"

He explained that because the Muir wall is one of the least climbed routes we would avoid possible climber congestion. Climbers above become particularly problematic; they can slow you down by getting in the way or, worse, drop things. A small carabineer, plunging straight down hundreds or thousands of feet, can cause serious damage and even death. I recalled how difficult it had been negotiating around climbers on the narrow ridge of the Matterhorn, and knew this climb took that challenge to another level. Passing another climber on a sheer wall is a dangerous enough proposition, let alone negotiating around the massive gear of two parties. Further complicating matters, our six-man team created our own "congestion" as we stood to be the largest to ever attempt this route.

It was September 3, 2005, and, after more than two years of planning, we finally made our way to Yosemite for the big event. We met as a team for coffee the next morning at sunrise to get an early start. How strange to be leaving the horizontal world for six whole days!

Our team had a few glitches. Ken had cracked his rib just days earlier. In addition, Scott had been fighting flu-like symptoms that were similar to the sinister, mosquito-borne West Nile Virus that had been found in the area. Fortunately, he had tested negative for it, and felt nearly recovered. Also, Scott had tweaked his wrist during a recent climb. He began to doubt if he would be able to join us. Neither Ken nor Scott ever go down with minor injuries, so I worried they'd mentioned their calamities at all—it must be serious! When Scott said his wrist felt healed, I wondered, "Is he just sucking it up, or did it really get better?" I preferred to think his wrist had miraculously healed, just as my ankle had prior to Kilimanjaro. With Scott seemingly at full capacity, Ken remained our biggest concern. We were relying heavily on him to shoulder the lion's share of the haul bag load. We would all need to pitch in and do our best. At least Kevin was injury free and without any issues, as far as we knew. As the guys wrapped up their discussion of recent wounds, I relished their spirit. No complaining, nor any false bravado from this group! Injuries had no sway over us.

After coffee, we headed to El Capitan Meadow to assemble and pack all our gear, food, clothes, haul and lead ropes, portaledges, etc. In addition to the standard gear, I brought along what looked like a pharmacy of medications, a blood pressure machine, a pulse oxymeter and, of course, Handiwipes! No way would I risk my life climbing, and then succumb to a simple infection. My negligence would impel guidebook authors to update their next edition with one more threat—*germs!* In the end, the haul bags, referred to as "pigs," felt like lead, and the load increased by 320 pounds when we added forty gallons of water.

Although the haul bags held all our essentials, Craig and I also wore small backpacks filled with our daily needs. Included in my pack was a week's worth of medication. Additionally, I kept a second week's supply in one of the haul bags, just in case. I could only imagine taking out my precious meds, bumping my arm and watching them tumble into the abyss. I not only had to be careful with the ropes and knots, but just as mindful when handling my lifesaving drugs, as they are as vital as any piece of equipment.

We made our way to the wall's base, lugging all our gear up a steep narrow trail. Although the approach lasted only forty minutes, my labored breath revealed the struggle to carry my share of the weight. As a wonderful distraction, several friends and supporters joined us on the trek to the base of the wall. TJ felt proud to share in this experience. It seemed so long ago that I was in this same valley regretfully pleading into the phone to her, "If I ever want to climb another mountain, don't let me." After farewell hugs and my requisite pre-climb butterflies, I positioned myself at the wall to begin. As much as I had been at ease with heights in all our training, I was now going to ascend 3,000 vertical feet, 2,000 vertical feet higher than I'd been on any other sheer rock face. Momentarily, I thought to myself, "I hope my adrenaline fires my heart rather than my nerves!"

We quickly ascended to the heart of El Cap, our first destination and the symbol of our climb. On the very first night, we were standing in the lobe of the heart, appropriately called Heart Ledges. This ledge, although narrow, was just long and wide enough for Craig and I to sleep head-to-toe on, which saved us setting up a hanging portaledge. Early the next morning, before rigging up for the next pitch, Craig divulged an emotional surprise. Though we were far from the highest point, we *were* at the climb's symbolic apex, the stone heart that I'd dreamed about for so long. Craig's wonderful secret involved a tribute to two young girls who represented the very essence of this climb.

First he presented me with a 2 x 3 laminated photo of Jennifer Eller, a spirited young girl who had fought a courageous battle with Leukemia, but ultimately lost. The photo captured her in action, tagging a competitor out at home base while serving as catcher in an All Star softball game. What made the photo so poignant was that Jenny looked completely healthy, yet not an ounce of blood in her body was her own, personifying the importance of blood donation. The night of her death, her father Dean promised he would not let her legacy die with her. He quit his thirty-year job as a mortgage banker to become a spokesperson for blood donation and later President of the California Blood Center. It was thanks to Dean and his team's efforts that we were able to orchestrate our Yosemite blood drive.

The next photo was of Brittany Stark, a thirteen-year-old girl I'd befriended back in December 1997. On the too-long transplant list waiting for a new heart, Brittany looked up to me as a source of hope after learning of my early climbing accomplishments. In fact, while waiting for a heart, she hung a newspaper clipping and photo of me atop Mt. Whitney in her hospital room as a source of inspiration for what she envisioned would be her own healthy and active future. Unfortunately Brittany's body gave out before a heart became available. Needless to say, she epitomized the need for an increase in organ donations. After a moment of sorrow and tears, I attached the small pictures to my backpack for the rest of climb. The girls' spirits provided the added strength and inspiration needed to reach my summit goal.

The first part of the climb was very steep, but less severely angled than the sheer and overhanging sections we would encounter higher up. In fact, the lower portion jetted out like a paw or foot holding up the rest of the wall. While the climbing remained quite challenging, there were occasional small, shelf-like protrusions where I could briefly stand, providing temporary relief from my harness while letting me relish a vista made for the gods.

Most climbing routes seem similar to road maps with one distinct difference; roads usually follow the path of least resistance, while routes up the face of El Cap do not. However, just as a roadmap twists and turns, so do many of the crack lines that ascend a wall. The line is not always straight, meaning there are sometimes areas that need to be traversed. Because we wanted to climb through "the heart," we modified our route, which forced us to make a lateral transition toward the Muir wall. Facing this section, the famous climber/writer Greg Child's words echoed in my head, "The only thing more abstract than climbing up a wall is to traverse it from one side to the other." I moved slowly, a bit timid, feeling ever so vulnerable. Even with protection, I knew if I fell, I could take a big swing and possibly even slam into the wall, which could cause as much damage as hitting the ground. My mental pictures became much too vivid and my imagination took flight. I could just visualize skin, bones . . . and a heart, dangling like a rag doll 1,000 feet up a wall on a rope the width of a forefinger. While this pendulum maneuver may create a cool visual effect, it was not what I needed replaying in my head. Fearful that my trepidation would paralyze me, I chased the "horror" show out of my mind. Coldly efficient, I focused exclusively on my skills. To my surprise, calmness ensued. Once I got beyond the traverse and the freaky, exposed moves, my newfound composure thrilled me. I had learned to trust the system.

Trust. Looking back, I had to put trust in the medical system—the doctors, equipment, and medications. It was the same with climbing. I put my trust in the guides, the gear and the ropes. My medical history also provided tools for coping with potentially risky exposure. Furthermore, my body has become accustomed to change and readily adapts. Just as I had adjusted to a constant barrage of medications, my eyes had adjusted to living on the vertical plane. Our systems are remarkably talented at coping, compensating, and self-adjusting, no matter what madness we impose on them.

When we were about one-third of the way up, the terrain began to angle even further skyward. Any remaining ledges were now just mere slivers, none wider than a few inches. Because we were tackling the wall one long pitch at a time, approximately 100 feet each, Craig and I were rarely together. We'd part in the morning, and often never see one another again until the end of the day. We did, though, check in via walkie-talkies. Craig asked how I was doing, while I made sure he didn't feel forgotten, as he was the team member most often left on his own. With each day, the hauling became a little easier due to less drag against the wall and increasingly lighter loads as we consumed water and food. I had cycles of being busy, interspersed with periods of waiting and rest; but, all in all, the days seemed to fly by. I delighted in the awesome feeling of being vertical—like a fly on the wall.

Four days into the climb, about 2,600 feet up, the cars that had first looked like toys, then like Tic Tacs, had become barely recognizable specs. With our walkie-talkies, we periodically checked in with our ever-enthusiastic and excited friends and supporters in the valley below, providing live updates that were posted on the Internet and also relayed to people at blood centers who eagerly followed the climb.

Words cannot describe the stunning sunrises and sunsets. Unfortunately, Craig worked during the sunsets because he was always the last person to the bivy site, not once arriving before nightfall. It was comforting to have the team around me, and tough to think of Craig far below, all by himself in the dark. He also had the daunting responsibility of making methodic sense of the tangle of gear, clipping and unclipping, tying and untying knots. I found it hard enough to handle such tasks in bright daylight with Scott and Kevin close by should I need guidance, and didn't envy Craig in his role. Yet Craig seemed to enjoy his role as the "cleaner." The challenge and sense of control melded well with his personality. Each night, after Craig arrived with the haul bags, we set up our camp, and before turning in we'd dine on tins of cold soup, which tasted amazingly delicious after a long, hard day of climbing.

Stillness and peace claimed the nights. After the long days of physical and mental exertion, sleep was deep. Craig and I had a double portaledge, so we were side-by-side, albeit head to toe so as not to upset the delicate balance of the artificial ledge. A portaledge is a fabric-covered platform surrounded by a metal frame, similar to a cot that is hung on the wall from a single point and has adjustable suspension straps. The other team members slept on their own portaledges, spread out six to ten feet above, below, or to the side of us, depending on our location on the wall. My friend Barbara contacted me via walkie-talkie from far below each night, and said our cluster of headlamps looked like a quaint little village of wall dwellers. Our team's nightly conversation was filled with lively fun, though I must admit I felt like the only girl at a testosterone-fueled slumber party.

In spite of the tremendous challenge of the climb, and as relaxing as sleeping on the wall became, the normally simple task of going to the bathroom made me feel like I was being potty trained all over again. Luckily, during the day I never had to pee. This is one of the advantages that my medications afford me.

Of course, the plus of being able to hold it all day is offset by the minus of needing to let it out later. As such, I was required to perform a rather balletic maneuver as much as six times a night. My daily practice of yoga came in handy, as I needed to balance carefully while I released the leg loops of my harness, pulled my pants down and did my business. Although I felt in control, Craig did not have the same level of confidence, because, frankly speaking, my toilet was his bed! It was a matter of aim, and since he didn't want me to mess our one and only refuge, he became a committed participant. Positioned closest to the wall with Craig on the outermost edge, I was able to support myself with one hand braced on to the trail of ropes supporting the bivy and use my other hand to carefully position a pee bottle directly underneath me. Craig would then sit up and grab onto my harness to steady me. Once I was done, Craig tightly secured the cap for my next session or, if full, carefully poured it out making sure not to rain on anyone below . . . at least in our party!

But the real challenge came when someone had to go "number two." Not that it was exactly announced, but when you ask, "Where's the toilet paper?" it's pretty obvious what's up. How it's done is in a makeshift toilet, more commonly known as a plastic grocery bag. When the deed is done, it's wrapped in a second plastic bag and put into a designated bucket or poop tube, which is attached to one of the haul bags and hauled up the entire climb as our team's porta-potty. Luckily, over the course of six days, I didn't have to go once. I had never been so delighted with constipation as a side effect of my medication!

One rule of thumb while climbing is that everything needs to be clipped into some kind of gear at all times. While organizing our bags and getting snacks out for the following day, Ken handed me a gallon jug of water. When I grabbed it, it was heavier than I expected, throwing me off balance and causing it to slip out of my fingers. For a moment my heart stopped. What flashed in my mind was that old urban myth about what happens to a penny when it is dropped from the top of the Empire State Building. We were well above the height of the Empire State Building, and the gallon jug of water weighed as much as nearly 1,300 pennies. Maybe one penny couldn't kill a person on the sidewalk below, but what I dropped would certainly be fatal to a climber caught in its downward path! We all held our breath while yelling "rock" desperately hoping no one stayed in the line of fire. After several long seconds, we could hear the sound of the plastic container exploding on an unoccupied portion of the rock far below.

Waking up each morning in the vertical world became as thrilling for me as standing atop a major peak. Imagine this: morning light reflected off the surrounding rock faces before slowly filling the valley below, a scene drawn from the position of a distant planet looking down at Earth. The temperature plummets just prior to sunrise, the coldest part of the day. Snuggled inside the cozy cocoon of my sleeping bag, I'd hear Scott in a bivy above us, firing up the small stove with hot water for morning coffee. Forget room service, this was so much better. Scott used fresh ground beans, filtered the piping hot liquid into my cup, covered it with a lid, tied a rope around the handle, and most fun of all, lowered it graciously to me so I could enjoy coffee in bed. If Scott ever decided to set up a chain of rope-and-pulley coffee stands, Starbucks would be out of business.

The final two pitches included an exciting, fully exposed ascent over what can best be described as a massive stone roof. This is a natural horizontal outcrop that extends out from the wall, leaving the person who is ascending hanging in midair. It was the climax of our amazing journey, so we took our time, savoring each suspended instant.

Once over the roof, the route dramatically levels off, with just one last segment requiring an awkward scramble to a safe zone. High spirits leaped even higher than the 3,000 feet we just climbed as I made my way up that final section. A small, straggly tree stood between my ultimate destination and me. Of course I became tangled in it, sending Michael and Scott into fits of merry laughter. Still, nothing could prevent me from finally untying my rope and standing on solid ground. I felt liberated!

Meanwhile, Craig worked hard with Ken to hoist the last three haul bags over the roof. To do this, Craig assumed the role of a human counterbalance, dangling 3,000 feet upside down, looking down at the world gone topsy-turvy with his feet pushing off under the roof, while pulling the bags to the top of the pitch. Insane hardly describes the image. Finally, about two hours later, Craig arrived at the top, the last man up.

A bubble wand appeared in his hand, and a gentle yet triumphant smile lit his face. This was the place where wishes came true. He then presented me with a shiny little object that he had secretly tucked away. It was a gold replica of El Cap, complete with the symbolic heart we had just climbed through meticulously embedded into the sheer face. The glimmering icon reflected all the hard work that went into this adventure, a welcome addition to the charms that continued to fill my mountain bracelet. But it wasn't about the charms themselves. I knew then that my bracelet, so full of life, had truly come to represent a life fulfilled.

The Heart of
the Matter

IN 1988, we stood on the volcanic rim of Mt. St. Helens, transfixed by the ash and devastation that surrounded us. This mountain, which had been one of the most beautiful and pristine in the area, had violently exploded eight years earlier, and was forever changed. Where trees had lifted their branches to the sky, only rubble remained. Sometimes we'd find ourselves knee-deep in ash. We had no way of knowing that, four years later, our lives would explode with similarly seismic fury. We did not know that we, too, would be changed forever.

We have since heard that new growth is beginning to flourish on Mt. St. Helens—rich, green vegetation and flowers opening to the sun. It's part of the cycle of life, and it is happening with us as well. The explosion that shook our lives fertilized opportunities for us to enjoy life in intriguing new ways. We've learned so much from nature: how the unexpected can force us to change direction, and how fresh possibilities can wait just beyond the most fearsome bends in the road.

Craig and I now live life with more conviction and intent; along with my new heart came a new purpose.

While we believe in seeing and creating beautiful moments each day, we have also learned that it's essential to look beyond our own selves, to recognize a higher purpose that each one of us can fulfill. We have many dreams, many mountains ahead of us to climb—but our true legacy is to help people become more aware and participate in blood, tissue, and organ donation. A courageous woman named Carol left behind her wish that her organs be donated. Her heart gave me a new beginning. The statistics are becoming more and more desperate.

According to the United Network for Organ Sharing (UNOS) and the U.S. Department of Health and Human Services, as of May 2007, there are more than 96,000 people across the United States in need of organ transplants and comparatively few donors. This discrepancy between supply and demand of organs for transplantation is growing at an alarming rate. For example, in 1995, the year of my transplant, the number of patients on the national waiting list was 41,179, of which only 19,369 (47%) received organs. As of December 2006, the waiting list had grown to 93,699, of which only 28,923 (31%) received organs. Put yourself in the shoes of someone desperately ill and facing these daunting odds. It doesn't have to be this way! Furthermore, this gap will continue to grow until people proactively participate by signing their donor card, state registry (if available), and discussing their decision with their family, all critical components of the donation process.

We have gained so much from the challenges we've faced, from the mountains we've climbed, and the people we've met on our incredible journey. I believe that Carol is smiling down on me, happy to know that she's given me a gift that will live on.

FRAIL TO FIT,
Kelly's Path to Building Strength

WHILE I have a background in nutrition, I do not claim to be an expert. As such, I am sharing my philosophy and what has proven to work for me.

Fortunately, I don't have to substitute flavor for healthfulness when it comes to the food I choose. I believe in healthful eating to maintain a healthy weight and create vitality. It's difficult to avoid the ubiquitous and aggressive assault from advertising on our consciousness as it relates to sensible eating, especially with respect to weight loss and fad diets. As we all know, extreme restrictions are not healthy or sustainable over the long term. As soon as the diet is over, the weight is added right back. Furthermore, this type of yo-yo behavior, dieting, and binge eating, creates havoc with ones metabolism, making it harder each time to lose weight. Eating is very individual, and the only way to establish and incorporate good dietary behaviors into your life is to find healthy foods that are satisfying and that you enjoy. The pathological patterns in our eating are easy to identify and fix, including mountainous portions, too many empty calories that do not provide satiety, consumption of high calorie liquid drinks (gourmet coffees, sugary soft drinks, juices), eating too many fats (good and bad), and last but not least, lack of consistent exercise. It comes down to a lifestyle, not a weekend warrior approach.

Exercise is as critical a component of good health as maintaining a proper diet. Like diet, exercise lowers our topmost health related risk factors: cancer, heart disease, and diabetes. Furthermore, it's essential for maintaining a healthy body weight; because muscle is "calorie hungry" (active tissue requiring energy), the more muscle you have, the more calories you'll burn even when you are sitting or sleeping. Fat is passive, and burns significantly fewer calories, thereby slowing the metabolism. In addition to maintaining a healthy weight, it's important to look at exercise as a cleanser, energizer, and stress releaser, rather than for the sake of vanity.

The human body is more of a miracle than we can fathom. One example is my new heart and it's response to exercise. It's fascinating that I have a back up system (adrenaline) to communicate with my heart, as it no longer receives direct information from my brain through nerves. Another one is the efficient process of metabolism. We gain weight not because our body is stubborn; we gain weight because the body has a certain need for nutrients, and once it is met, the extra calories turn to fat. Excess fuel (food) equals excess fat. The body's brilliant survival mechanism is often overlooked in our culture because most of us have not had a need to tap into it; instead, we have the opposite problem, a plethora of foods and ever-increasing portions, a less physical lifestyle, resulting in a higher intake than our body needs and, as a result, a rising obesity rate.

Think of a car. When you don't have gas in your car, it poops out and stops. But your body without food goes into survival mode; it begins to tap into its reserves to keep its organs functional. This can and does save lives. Medical procedures, especially if invasive or surgical, require tremendous energy demands on the body to recover and repair tissue, yet it was during these times that I would be required to fast up to twelve hours. The fasting is done to avoid having food and liquid in the stomach, which could be vomited and aspirated during the induction of anesthesia. The fasting period, when combined with the procedure and recovery time, would often mean a full twenty-four hours without food. Similarly, during climbs or long treks I have gone extended periods without food, resulting in a tremendous imbalance where my energy output exceeded the level and rate it was restored. Fortunately, I did better than the car without gas; I was able to count on my body's instinctive ability to utilize reserves to sustain me until I could replenish myself and, at the same time, maintain my strength. The metabolic process is the body's powerhouse that drives our energy and vitality. It is one of the many advanced efficiencies that enables us to build and maintain muscle mass, maintain a stable and healthy weight, and helps us avoid disease.

I feel very fortunate to be healthy, but I didn't wait for it—I worked to make it happen.

Most Frequently Asked Questions

*N*ote: *This is what I do. This information is not intended to serve as a replacement for the advice of your physician.*

Q. How much fat do you have in your diet?

A. I eat limited fats; generally 15 percent of my daily diet is fat and only from good sources (monounsaturated and polyunsaturated fats), which include avocados, nuts and seeds, olives/olive oil, and salmon (omega 3s). I never buy sauces, dips, or dressings that exceed a total of 3 grams of any kind of fat. I also avoid trans fats and saturated fats. Fats are important, because they aid in the absorption of fat-soluble vitamins. However, reducing total fat can help lower your risk of heart disease, which is obviously my goal.

Q. How much protein do you eat?

A. I eat a fair amount of protein, approximately 25 to 30 percent of my caloric intake. Proteins are essential to our diet as they build and repair tissue. Naturally, the higher demand you put on your body, as with surgery or exercise, the more "repair" is needed, and therefore, the higher the required intake. In addition to plant proteins, I eat lean sources including egg whites, skinless chicken breast, fish (including wild salmon), white turkey, and nonfat dairy. Also, because of my medication, lean proteins work well with an often irritated or sensitive stomach. While soy is a good source, I cannot tolerate it, as it acts as a synthetic estrogen and, for me, causes an allergic type reaction.

Q. Do you watch your carbohydrate intake?
A. Yes, to make sure I get enough. The largest portion of my diet comes from carbohydrates, roughly 55 percent. The main purpose of carbohydrates is to provide energy to cells. Certain tissues, such as red blood cells, and some parts of the brain derive almost all of their energy from carbohydrates. Furthermore, because they are the most readily available energy source, I rely on them for fuel to exercise. I do pay attention to the Glycemic Index in choosing carbohydrates, opting for low GI carbs (the ones that produce only small fluctuations in my blood sugar), which are claimed to have long-term health benefits relating to reducing heart disease and diabetes. I stay away from all processed foods, crackers, prepackaged pastas and cereals because most often they are stripped of fiber and contain high fructose corn syrup. If I eat sugar, I balance it with a protein and a good fat, like nonfat frozen yogurt with almonds. As far as fruits and vegetables, I consciously take advantage of local seasonal varieties, which provide me with plenty of choice nearly year round.

Q. Do you eat nutrition or fitness bars?
A. Rarely, and only if whole foods are not available. I am much more satisfied with a piece of fruit, a cup of soup, or a slice of turkey. Most of the bars are concentrated in calories and usually quite high in fat. On occasion, as with a trek lasting more than three hours where food is not easily accessible, I will eat an energy bar.

Q. Do you ever stray from your diet?

A. Very rarely, such as peanut M&Ms during our thirteen-hour Matterhorn climb. I don't take a vacation from my health. There is no need to; I like what I eat. Refraining from desserts, for instance, doesn't require any willpower. I don't eat them because I don't want them. I look at it the way a devout vegetarian would relate to a steak. It's not an occasion-related decision; it's a cornerstone of my lifestyle.

Q. How do you order in a restaurant?

A. Most good restaurants are generally happy to accommodate my requests. I order foods prepared simply, meaning steamed, broiled or grilled, sauce on the side, or pizza without cheese. I never order sautéed or grilled vegetables because they usually arrive swimming in oil. I avoid soups because often they are high in fat and sodium. In ordering salads, I always order dressing on the side and make sure there are no croutons or cheese. If the dressing is questionable, I order balsamic vinegar on the side.

If there is a challenge, it's usually due to a language barrier in a foreign country when I try to explain how I want my food prepared. Usually, I will do my homework beforehand and have a note in the language of the country I am visiting, explaining my dietary restrictions. Or, I'll find someone who speaks English who can help. If all else fails, I show my scar and most people get it!

Q. Do you ever overeat?

A. Consume large quantities, yes. Overeat, not really. I eat what my body needs. I do find the "super sizing" trend in restaurant portions ridiculous, and often take half the food away because it's simply unappetizing to look at. If it's something I love, I will immediately take half away to avoid being irresponsible because, like most, if it's there I will nibble. If it's not there, I don't think about it.

Q. Do you take supplements?
A. I do my best to get an adequate intake of nutrients from food as I choose colorful fruits and vegetables that are loaded with vitamins, minerals, and fiber. However, to make sure, I take Omega 3s, a magnesium/calcium supplement, and a Vitamin B complex. I take vitamins six days a week, with one day off. Also, because I am small, I take half the prescribed adult dose. I do not subscribe to the theory that if a little is good, a lot must be great.

Q. Are you conscience about water intake?
A. Extremely. Staying hydrated helps me function at my optimum level and is especially important given my medications and exercise. Water is required for basic physiological functions including delivery of nutrients to tissues, maintaining blood pressure and flushing the body of toxins. I view water as a means to nourishment and purification.

Knowing proper hydration is critical to health and fitness, Craig and I created an interactive tool to help individuals quantify, achieve, and maintain optimal hydration. It's called the HydraCoach, and came about as a result of our experience, vision, and personal need. Visit: www.hydracoach.com *for more information.*

Q. Do you drink coffee or alcohol?
A. Both. I love my morning coffee, but I limit it to two cups a day. It revs up my engine, kicks starts my heart. This especially helps me with cardiovascular exercise as it induces an increased heart rate, which is delayed by lack of nerves from my transplant. Naturally, I do not order decadent fat and calorie-laden coffees. As for alcohol, I drink only wine. I have a glass every evening before dinner. Moderation is the key! Research has shown benefit to drinking wine or alcohol for the heart, including the role of antioxidants and an increase in HDL ("good") cholesterol. Besides, it's a treat, it tastes good and it takes the edge off!

Q. What's the most common question you are asked?
A. *I am often asked, "What do you eat?" It's as if I have some dietary secret that keeps weight off. What keeps weight off is not what I eat; it's exercise and what I don't eat!*

Q. How often do you exercise?
A. *Every day. Five to six days a week I do yoga for ninety minutes; I rock climb in a climbing gym three times per week and, on my rest days, I hike or walk. As a rule of thumb, I never take more than forty-eight hours off from strenuous exercise.*

Q. How do you stay disciplined when it comes to exercise?
A. *I feel better when I move; it's as simple as that. Having an impaired cardiac output, exercise helps facilitate my circulation by keeping my fingers and toes warm as well as moving around the toxic residue from my medications. Secondly, my exercise is a positive distraction from my ongoing health-related issues. I especially find an "escape" with rock climbing and yoga because they are both mindful.*

Q. What time of day do you work out?
A. *I have always been a morning person and exercise immediately after I get out of bed. The time of my workout is especially significant since my illness because I prefer to exercise during my drug trough, the period when my drugs are at their lowest level in my bloodstream. During this period, I feel better, stronger, and have more endurance. Furthermore, several studies have shown that people who work out first thing in the morning are more likely to stick with their exercise routine due to fewer distractions. This has definitely been my experience.*

Q. Do you push yourself every day?
A. *Most of the time I push my edge because I use my energy level and fitness to gauge to my health. I fear going backwards*

medically, so I try to do my best every day. However, I do listen to my inner teacher and respond accordingly. At times, my body needs more nurturing, and by backing off I have been able to prevent injuries as well as psychological "burnout."

Q. Do you do cardiovascular (aerobic) exercise?
A. I hike or take a vigorous walk. The hikes I do are in the foothills, which provide steep and challenging terrain. However, initially after my transplant, I had a low tolerance level for cardiovascular exercise. With time, I added endurance and intensity. It's helpful to be goal-oriented, adhering to a plan that allows for safe progression by giving my body at least a few weeks to adjust before progressing to a new level. For example, I took baby steps with walking, starting with flatland before adding hills, blocks before miles, miles and hills before mountains. As with any exercise, I find it's important not to judge but to honor your body during the process.

Q. Do you do strength training?
A. Yes, I think it is very important, especially in my situation. Strong muscles pluck oxygen from the blood much more efficiently than weak ones, which mean less stress on my heart. Furthermore, strong muscles are better at soaking up sugar in the blood and helping the body stay sensitive to insulin. This keeps the blood sugar in check, thereby preventing type-2 diabetes.

Initially after my illness, I joined a full-service gym and worked out five days a week, primarily lifting free weights. I started out very weak and very skinny, yet over time I was able to build some muscle strength. After about three years, and at a time when I was beginning to lose my drive, a new yoga studio opened nearby. It was a good transition. The weight lifting had given me a foundation, which helped me with yoga. Yoga quickly became my new passion. Because health is my primary focus, I liked that the poses work the body from the inside out rather than outside in, which happens in a gym. In 2000, after a few years bouncing around between different types of yoga, I switched exclusively to Ashtanga. Ashtanga is a vigorous athletic style of yoga that detoxifies the body and builds strength, flexibility, and stamina. The primary series, which is the most practiced in the United States, includes about seventy-five poses that take anywhere from an hour-and-a-half to two hours to complete, beginning with Sun Salutations and moving on to standing poses, seated poses, inversions, and backbends before relaxation. Also, what I love about Ashtanga is that the focus lies in the "practice," removing the attachment to doing the pose. In other words, it is not outcome driven. This "practice and all is coming" philosophy I have been able to apply on my yoga mat and to all aspects of my life.

Q. What is easier physically, hiking or climbing?
A. *They are very different. Climbing is more technical, mentally challenging, and a full body workout. Yet, because my energy is more evenly dispersed between my upper, core, and lower body, it is less taxing on my heart. Hiking for long periods of time, and in high altitudes, is much more difficult due to my compromised cardiac output.*

Q. Do you still exercise when you don't feel well?
A. *Unless I am sick, have a temperature, or have had an invasive procedure, I go to yoga. At such times, I listen to my body and exercise accordingly. For example, when I had a blood pressure medication added, I would get dizzy with inversions (going upside down), so I didn't do them until I stabilized. Still, I was able to do 85 to 90 percent of the practice. For me, it's about showing up and doing something.*

About the Author

KELLY PERKINS was born in 1961 and raised in California and later in Nevada, in Lake Tahoe. She attended University of Oregon as well as San Francisco State University, studying both Health Sciences as well as Dietetics. She moved to Southern California in 1986 where she had a career as a real estate appraiser. In 1987 she married her college sweetheart Craig.

In September 1992, Kelly was diagnosed with cardiomyopathy; she had caught a virus that infected her heart. Just after three years, and just prior to Kelly's heart completely failing, she received a heart transplant at the University of California at Los Angeles Medical Center. Shortly after, Kelly returned to the mountains, joyfully transcending her life threatening illness to become a world renowned mountain climber who used each peak and summit to passionately advocate for the life saving gift of organ donation.

Along with Craig, Kelly is cofounder and the "heart beat" behind HydraCoach, a product developed for the medical, sporting, and health-minded community. Currently, Kelly continues to climb as well as speak to promote organ, blood, and tissue donation.

Kelly's journey has gained international media attention: Feature stories have appeared in the *Los Angeles Times, USA Today,* the *New York Times,* the *San Francisco Chronicle, SELF, McCall's, Cooler Magazine,* and even the *Japan Times Weekly.* She has also appeared on ABC, NBC, CBS, and CNN radio and numerous television programs, including *ABC News with Peter Jennings, The Today Show, EXTRA,* and *Good Morning America with Charlie Gibson.*